D0208587

The Plan

Twelve months to renew Britain

Douglas Carswell and Daniel Hannan

First published in Great Britain 2008 by Douglas Carswell and Daniel Hannan

Copyright © Douglas Carswell and Daniel Hannan

The right of Douglas Carswell and Daniel Hannan to be identified as the authors of this work has been asserted by them in accordance with the Copyright, Designs & Patents Act, 1988.

A catalogue record for this book is available from the British Library.

ISBN: 978-0-9559799-0-3

All rights reserved. No part of this publication may be reproduced or transmitted in any form or by any means, electronic or mechanical including photocopying, recording or information storage or retrieval system, without the prior permission in writing of the publishers.

This book is sold subject to the condition that it shall not by way of trade or otherwise be lent, resold, hired out, or otherwise circulated without the publishers' prior consent in writing in any form of binding or cover other than that in which it is published and without a similar condition being imposed on the subsequent purchaser.

To the size of a state there is a limit, as there is to plants, animals and implements, for they can none of them retain their facility when they are too large.

ARISTOTLE

When the government fears the people, there is liberty. When the people fear the government, there is tyranny.

THOMAS JEFFERSON

A country does not have to be judged to be fit for democracy, rather it has to become fit through democracy.

AMARTYA SEN

The delegation of particular technical tasks to separate bodies, while a regular feature, is yet the first step by which a democracy progressively relinquishes its powers.

F A HAYEK

About the authors

DANIEL HANNAN is a writer and journalist. He has worked as a leader writer for *The Daily Telegraph* since 1996, and has also written for *The Wall Street Journal*, *The Sunday Telegraph*, *The Times*, *The Australian*, *The Catholic Herald*, *Arena*, *The Guardian*, *Freedom Today* and *The Spectator*. He contributes regularly to a number of Continental newspapers, including the German daily *Die Welt* and the Swiss political magazine *Weltwoche*. His books include *Time for a Fresh Start in Europe* (1993) *A Guide to the Amsterdam Treaty* (1997), *The Euro: Bad for Business* (1998), *The Challenge of the East* (1999), *What if Britain Votes No?* (2002) and *The Case for EFTA* (2004). He has been a Conservative MEP for South East England since 1999, and was re-selected in top position for the 2004 and 2009 European elections. He blogs every day at www.hannan.co.uk

DOUGLAS CARSWELL has been Conservative MP for Harwich and Clacton since 2005. He previously worked in fund management, and before that in commercial television. Immediately prior to the 2005 General Election, he worked for the Conservative Party's Policy Unit helping prepare the manifesto. In 2008, he sponsored a Private Members' Bill to allow parliamentary legislation to be tabled directly by members of the public through petitions. He has also led the campaign to replace Speaker Martin. He has written for *The Mail on Sunday*, *The Daily Telegraph*, *The Sunday Times* and *The Financial Times*. His publications include *Direct Democracy* (2002) and *Paying for Localism* (2004). He blogs every day at www.TalkCarswell.com

Contents

Introduction

The British state is failing. It can't deliver even the most basic services competently. We have the highest prisoner population in Europe, and one of the highest crime rates. Our schoolchildren compare dismally with similarly aged pupils in other countries and in previous generations. Our healthcare system is more likely to kill its charges than any other in the developed world. Our roads are choked, our railways crumbling, our airports unbearable. Our borders are, to all intents and purposes, wide open.

This is not to say that *Britain* is failing. We still lead most of our lives outside the direction of the government, and we do so, by and large, successfully. We are an inventive people: bold, restless and quizzical. King's College Cambridge has produced more winners of the Nobel Prize than has France. British enterprise means that, in general, our economy tends to grow, our existence to become more comfortable, our ambitions to become wider. Cheap flights, broadband, iPhones: these things have transformed our lives. Yet no government task force, no focus group, would ever have dreamed them up beforehand.

Indeed, it is the contrast between our dealings with the state and our dealings with everyone else that makes the failures of the British government so painfully apparent. When we book a holiday or go shopping, we can do so with a few clicks of a mouse. Compare that experience to applying for planning permission – let alone trying to get your child into a particular school.

CONCORDIA UNIVERSITY LIBRARY
PORTLAND, OR 97211

Plenty of devoted, clever and benign people work for the government. But the system serves to smother their individual virtues. Our schools don't simply underperform; they systematically mask that underperformance through manipulated examination grades. Our hospitals don't simply fail to cure people; they often infect them with diseases unrelated to their original complaints. Our prisons don't simply turn inmates away from reoffending; they make it more likely. Ponder the extraordinary fact that many convicts become addicted to drugs *while in prison*, and thus wholly in the hands of the state.

Meanwhile, more than 200,000 Britons emigrate every year; more than 300,000 foreigners settle in their place, many of them illictly. For the state cannot even discharge its elemental function: to secure the national territory.

Almost worse than the failure is the accompanying despair. People are not simply resigned to the malfunctioning of government: they have given up on any prospect of improvement. The promises made by politicians no longer even register: they are dismissed as a kind of electoral white noise. The country depicted by ministers – gleaming hospital wards, record A-level results, patrolling policemen – bears no relation to the one that voters see around them. As in the Soviet Union, people have come to operate in parallel worlds: the virtual world of official pamphlets and politicians' speeches, and the real one.

'I find the country bleeding, nay, almost dying,' Oliver Cromwell told MPs in 1644. What made him angry was not simply that people were suffering, but that Parliament was part of the problem. 'The People are dissatisfied in every corner of the Nation,' he raged, 'all men laying at our doors the non-performance of these things that had been promised'.

Today, people are not so much dissatisfied as fatalistic. No one expects any party to cut taxes, make public services work for their customers, reverse the flow of illegal migration or restore Britain's independence. Voters half sense that some politicians would like to do these things; but they know in their bones that the system is loaded against reform. 'Nothing ever really changes,' people protest; and, in a sense, they are right. Elected representatives have progressively ceded their powers to self-interested and inert bureaucracies – in Brussels as much as in Whitehall. With the best will in the world, there is remarkably little that politicians *can* change. Small wonder that fewer and fewer people vote: as matters stand, abstention is a rational decision.

Things don't have to be this way. Other countries give meaningful power to their citizens, both as consumers of government services and as voters. In Britain, too, the rise of the quango state and the decline of Parliament are relatively recent phenomena. What's done can be undone.

This book is written by two politicians who know at first hand how weak are the institutions of contemporary democracy in Britain, and how intense is the consequent sense of anger and impotence on the doorstep.

What follows is a plan to make the state accountable once more to its people. We propose a number of related initiatives: placing the criminal justice system under locally elected Sheriffs; making local councils self-financing; making healthcare answerable to patients, and education to parents; returning social security to counties and cities; withdrawing from the European Union; replacing prime ministerial patronage with open parliamentary hearings; tackling judicial activism; introducing local and national referendums.

We set out, in some detail, how an incoming government could achieve these ends within a single 12-month legislative session, so transforming forever the relationship between state and citizen. In one way, Parliament would be stronger: it would take substantial powers back from human rights judges, quangos, ministers and Eurocrats. In another, it would be weaker, having ceased to regulate matters that ought properly to be left to local authorities or, better yet, private individuals.

In a sense, though, our specific proposals matter less than the belief that infuses them: that people should control their own destinies; that the state should be the servant of the citizen; that power should be diffused; that decisions should be taken as closely as possible to the people they affect.

If you think these sentiments sound platitudinous, read on, and you will see quite how far modern government has drifted from them. Power to the people is a perennial slogan of both Left and Right. Actually delivering it will mean a revolution the like of which our country has not known.

Part One
The state of failure

Why everyone hates politicians

Did you vote at the last election? Statistically, you probably didn't. Sixty-four per cent of those who had taken the trouble to register in advance of the most recent poll – the council elections of May 2008 – chose to stay at home on the day. Turnout at local elections since 1996 has averaged 35.4 per cent. Participation at general elections, as we shall see, is also plummeting, reaching its lowest level since the universal franchise in 2001.

But let's say that you were in the 36 per cent: you are, after all, sufficiently interested in politics to have bought this book. If so, cast your mind back to polling day. Recall the moment when the ballot paper slid from your fingers into the black tin box. What exactly did you think your vote would achieve? Did you hope it would determine which school your child attended? Would it improve your local hospital? Would it lower your taxes or place more police on your street? Would it prevent an unpopular local housing development or determine the site of an incinerator? No? Then why were you voting?

Perhaps you felt a sense of civic obligation. Perhaps you are old enough to remember when ballots still had an impact on some of the issues listed

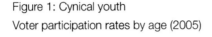

Figure 1: Cynical youth
Voter participation rates by age (2005)

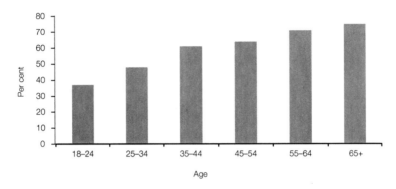

above. After all, voters over 65 were twice as likely to vote at the last general election as those under 25. It's not that pensioners are better citizens; it's that they grew up when Parliament was sovereign, and when elections determined the country's future. Their outlook recalls an era before politicians had parcelled out their powers to judges, civil servants, quangos and Eurocrats. Unless something is done to restore meaning and purpose to the ballot, turnout will continue to fall actuarially to a level commensurate with Parliament's present powerlessness.

Consider the statistics in Figure 1. Never before has there been such a sharp age disparity in turnout. It won't do to put it down to youthful apathy – the facile explanation traditionally reached for by columnists ('why won't they look up from *Manhunt 2* for long enough to show some interest?') The interesting question is not why younger people *don't* vote, but why older people *do*. On a raw cost-benefit analysis – the effort of filling in a ballot paper versus any consequential impact on your life – it is the abstainer who is behaving rationally.

It is not politics that leaves younger voters cold, so much as *elections*. Young people will turn out in large numbers to demonstrate about, say, trade justice. But they have accurately clocked that most of the questions they care about are beyond their votes – trade policy, for example, is determined by unelected European Commissioners.

Figure 2: Why bother? Turnout at general elections 1959–2005

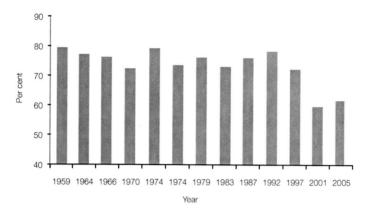

More immediate issues, too, have been lifted out of the democratic process. Human rights judges determine school uniform codes. The National Institute for Health and Clinical Excellence (NICE) arbitrates our access to medical treatment. Regional quangos tell us where to build our houses. Individual police chiefs decree local drugs policies.

Small wonder that fewer and fewer people bother to vote. It's not that they are apathetic. It's that they can see that their MPs and councillors have less impact on them than have the Learning and Skills Council, the Food Standards Agency, the Health and Safety Executive, the Financial Services Authority, the Equality Commission, the Child Support Agency and a thousand other quangos stretching up to the European Commission.

The fall in turnout mirrors almost precisely the rise of these agencies, as Figure 2 illustrates.

The complaints that a politician hears most often on the doorstep – 'you're all the same', 'you make promises but you never deliver', 'it doesn't matter how I vote, nothing ever changes' – are, to a single approximation, true. With the best will in the world, there is less and less that a politician *can* deliver.

This in turn helps explain another worrying trend: the public's growing disdain for politicians. As MPs have lost the power to ameliorate their constituents' circumstances, so they have forfeited their constituents' respect. Ceasing to be authoritative, they have become contemptible.

According to a survey by the Committee on Standards in Public Life, only 29 per cent of people trust politicians to tell the truth, as against 93 per cent who trust doctors and 84 per cent who trust head teachers. A YouGov poll in *The Daily Telegraph* in February 2008 showed that only four per cent of people believe that MPs put the country before themselves, and an astonishing 79 per cent agree with the statement: 'Most MPs use public office to make money improperly.'

While a measure of cynicism towards the political class is a feature of most democracies, the current level of distrust is unprecedented. We have reached the stage where, in a reversal of 200 years of political thinking, the mere fact of having been elected to office is seen as a disqualification. One of Gordon Brown's most popular early initiatives was his appointment of four non-politicians – a former CBI chief, a doctor, a retired admiral and a UN bureaucrat – to his ministry. According to another YouGov poll in *The Daily Telegraph*, voters applauded his decision by 56 to 19 per cent.

This is, on the face of it, a curious finding. You would think that someone who depends on our votes would be thought of as less remote, more accountable, than someone who doesn't. But here we reach the crux. People no longer regard the electoral process as anything to do with them. They see politicians as a separate caste.

Following the 2004 London and European elections – which, like all recent elections, were marked by apathy, anger and abstention – the Electoral Commission embarked on a major qualitative study to explain the electorate's attitude towards its representatives. The findings of its focus groups were, in the curious way that these things sometimes are, both predictable and shocking. People felt wholly disconnected from their politicians. They spoke of them almost as one would speak of an occupying power. To quote from the Electoral Commission's summary:

The language used by respondents throughout the groups illustrates the extent to which people do not regard politicians as their representatives, the champions of their interests, but as a privileged and distant elite, in their own world and with next to no understanding of the lives or ordinary people. The catch-all use of 'they' is applied indiscriminately.

This language seems more fitted to a dictatorship than a democracy. Think how aptly the above paragraph would apply to, say, the *apparatchiks* of the Soviet bloc. They, too, were thought to inhabit their own world. The country they described in their official propaganda – one with soaring production, full quotas and regular elections – bore no relation to that which their subjects could see around them. The attitude of voters towards politics in contemporary Britain is disquietingly similar to that of the captive peoples of the Comecon states: sullen, cynical, fatalistic.

How can this be when British politicians are obliged repeatedly to re-apply for their jobs through open elections?

The answer is staring us in the face. The British politician is no longer able to discharge his primary function. He cannot effect meaningful change in his constituents' lives. He has therefore ceased to be a vessel for popular will. No longer an agent of change, he has become a parasite.

Virtual government

Why does nothing ever change? Why are politicians unable to deliver the promises they make at election time? Why can't ministers carry out even the most obvious and uncontentious reforms to their departments?

It is assuredly not for want of trying. No Home Secretary *wants* prisoners to be absconding on a weekly basis. No education secretary *wants* a quarter of 16-year-olds to be functionally illiterate. No health secretary *wants* hospitals to be places where patients die of infections unrelated to their original condition. But they find that they cannot simply decree change. The state has become so large and unwieldy, the number of officials benefiting from the *status quo* so great, that no single minister, be he the most energetic in Whitehall, can refashion it.

For example, Labour's 1997 election manifesto promised: 'We will work towards the elimination of mixed-sex wards.' There is no doubt that the party meant to do precisely that, and its 2001 manifesto repeated the pledge: 'Mixed sex wards will be abolished.' But in January 2008, the health minister, Lord Darzi of Denham, announced that the policy was 'an aspiration that cannot be met'.

Similarly, every Home Secretary promises to reduce the amount of police form-filling. In 2002, David Blunkett committed himself to a 'bonfire of the paperwork'. In 2005, Charles Clarke announced that there was 'too much bureaucracy' in the police service, and promised to 'cut red tape'. Today, as we shall see in the next section, there is more paperwork in the police than ever.

In each of these cases, ministers have tugged at levers only to find that they are loose, jabbed at buttons that have long since been disconnected. Pledges given in good faith could not, in the event, be fulfilled: the machinery of state had become too inert to respond. This of course makes voters cynical; but, equally, it makes politicians cynical.

Once he realises that he cannot effect meaningful change, the minister tries instead to show that he is active. He sends out blizzards of press releases announcing Initiatives and Zones and Action Plans and New Deals. As in the old Soviet bloc, these decrees engender a certain amount of paperwork, but are not really expected or intended to have any practical consequences.

Tony Blair is perhaps the politician who best expressed the virtual nature of contemporary politics. In the run-up to the 2001 election, he wrote a memo that was later leaked, in which he explained that Labour needed some 'eye-catching initiatives' in order to regain public support.

The memo contained one sentence which bears particular contemplation: 'We also need a far tougher rebuttal or, alternatively, action.' Blair had grasped that, in the contemporary political climate, rebuttal *is* action – or, at least, as close to action as anyone expects. Presentation and practice have become blurred. Initiatives can be announced and re-announced – marching thugs to cash points, deep-cleaning hospitals, cracking down on illegal immigrants – and, by the time it becomes clear that nothing has changed, we are on to the next sound bite, the next headline. It is as though we inhabit the world of Descartes' malicious demon, the imaginary spirit that could define our reality by controlling our senses.

Blair's little *aperçu* was the neatest encapsulation of a post-modern politician's approach to post-modern politics. And in its own terms, it worked: its author was handsomely re-elected twice. But the country has paid a price in unprecedented political disenchantment.

Tony Blair was unusual in spelling out the extent to which policy-making had become presentational. But he did not cause the problem; he simply mastered the science of exploiting it. He understood, and he taught MPs on both sides of the aisle, that, in the absence of real power, appearance is all.

Even before Blair's election, legislation was becoming declamatory. The late Thatcher and Major years had seen a slew of laws whose chief purpose was to present their supporters in a good light: the Dangerous Dogs Act, the Football Spectators Act, the War Crimes Act. Tony Blair began his ministry with a spectacular example of the genre: the Firearms Act, passed in the aftermath of the Dunblane massacre. No one argued that such regulation would have prevented the atrocity. No one made a convincing case against the official recommendation: that pistols should be kept under lock at registered gun clubs. That was not really the point. The chief purpose of the Bill was to allow its supporters to show how upset they were about the murdered children and, by implication, to suggest that their opponents did not care as much as they did.

As Blair put it in a speech to his activists:

Conservative MPs complain that our response has been 'emotional'. Well, if they had been in that gym, if they had talked to those parents, sitting on those tiny chairs where once their children sat, they would have been emotional too. I believe we should ban the private ownership and possession of handguns.

The implication could hardly have been less subtle. Banning handguns was not a proportionate remedy to an identified problem. It was an act of public compassion, and anyone who voted against was somehow lacking in respect for the dead.

Not all legislation is declamatory, of course. But even on the occasions when a law will have real impact, politicians find it hard to break the habit of being mainly interested in where they are seen to stand. Ministers protest against post office closures in their own constituencies while supporting the closure programme nationally, and no one thinks it odd. Catholic politicians negotiate a dispensation allowing them to vote against embryo legislation, but only on the understanding that their votes will not affect its passage.

And why not? The longer they spend in politics, the clearer it becomes to them that, for all the fond ideals they began with, they cannot really alter anything that matters.

The state is running at capacity

Here is a list of recent news stories, drawn more or less at random from the press.

- 15 million people have their child benefit data lost in the post
- A government facility infects the national herd with foot and mouth
- 300,000 patients' prescriptions forms are lost
- Prisoners are absconding at a rate of more than one a week
- Holidaymakers are grounded by a technical breakdown in the passport agency
- Student loan payouts are delayed
- Poor people are forced to repay tax credits which they were wrongly allocated
- Discs containing information on British drivers are mislaid in Iowa
- Five million tax self-assessment forms go astray
- Thousands of newly qualified doctors are unable to find posts because of the failure of a new NHS computer system
- A-level grades are assigned erroneously because of errors at the Qualifications and Curriculum Authority
- Computer glitches in the benefits office have allowed £1.6 billion in welfare fraud

This last story could apply, *mutatis mutandis*, to virtually every organ of government. The past six years have seen massive and expensive IT failures at the Immigration Service, the Inland Revenue, the Post Office, the National Insurance Contributions Office and the Prison Service. Just as inevitable, just as inexorable, are the costly debacles involving consultants and public–private partnerships.

The cases listed are not examples of intrinsically wrong policies – though, as we shall see, there is no shortage of these either. Rather, they are straightforward failures of management. Nor will it do to put them down to occasional mistakes: their sheer quantity points to systemic failure rather than isolated human error.

So what is going wrong? Why does the state fail?

The answer is that modern government is already running at capacity. It has taken too much on. It is literally unable to assume new functions and discharge them efficiently.

Even during the early days of the planned state, some observers could see the problem. Foremost among them was Friedrich Hayek. His 1944 *magnum opus, The Road to Serfdom,* is often thought of as a work of timeless political philosophy. But it is in some ways better understood as a product of its time, a campaigning tract, a warning against pursuing the kind of collectivism in Britain that prevailed in contemporary Europe, then largely under fascist or communist control. Quite apart from the traditional liberal objection – that the corporatist state was incompatible with personal freedom – Hayek could see that centralisation was unsuited to the complexities of modern administration:

There would be no difficulty about efficient control or planning were conditions so simple that a single person or board could effectively survey all the relevant facts. It is only as the factors which have to be taken into account become so numerous that it is impossible to take a synoptic view of them that decentralisation becomes imperative.

Hayek's warning went unheeded. The exigencies of full mobilisation prompted an unprecedented extension of state control in Britain: nationalisation, tax rises, identity cards, rationing. When the Second World War came to an end, Whitehall made no move to relinquish the powers that it had seized on a supposedly contingent basis. On the contrary, the state of mind fostered by wartime propaganda – that we all had to make sacrifices, that we should unquestioningly obey officials, that it was unpatriotic to complain – made possible the post-war health, education, housing and welfare settlements, all based on the assumption that the government ought to take the lead in most aspects of life. And, of course, as technology progressed, as life became more complicated, as the state became engorged, it became harder and harder to 'survey all the relevant facts'.

The curious thing is that, although the state has grown more or less uninterruptedly since Hayek's day, its expansion has not been accompanied by any rise in doctrinal support for central planning. These days, few mainstream politicians argue for the nationalisation of large chunks of the economy, for prices and incomes policies, or for a state-run housing sector. Where the 1940s settlement still persists – notably in the fields of social security, education and, above all, healthcare – it does so more from institutional inertia, vested interests and fear of change than because of a first-principles attachment to central control.

The experience of state control, whether in its Western European form of the mixed economy or in its Eastern European form of socialism, has convinced most observers that it doesn't work: it diminishes freedom, prosperity and democracy while doing great harm to the people it was most intended to help. Yet, so far, few commentators have followed through the logic of this failure. The reason that the state was bad at building cars, operating airlines or rationing food is not that it was trying to do the wrong things; it is that governments are too large and unwieldy to do *anything* especially well.

It is worth exploring some of the structural reasons why this is so.

Small is beautiful

Hayek's creed was more revolutionary than he realised. He had confined his critique to politics. But, in subsequent decades, people began to appreciate that Hayek's analysis was capable of far broader application.

Hayek had drawn a distinction between two sorts of politicians with different approaches to administration. Those whom he called 'rational constructivists' saw it as the duty of public men to lead, to administer, to lay down what worked best. Their approach led, in its most extreme form, to what he called the two strains of socialism: Marxism and fascism. But in its milder and more common form, it lay behind all state planning.

On the other hand were those he called 'evolutionary rationalists': those who were more sceptical of the ability of big organisations to deliver, and who tended to see the role of government as being confined to ensuring that the rule of law prevails, that property is protected and that the national territory is defended against foreign invasion. British political development, until relatively recently, tended to follow this second school: our politicians were empirical, liberal and sceptical. The state they administered was limited in its ambitions. Our legal system was based on the inherited folkright of common law, not on a series of top-down statutes. We disliked and mistrusted the Continental desire to regulate, order and conscript. Our pamphleteers used 'Jacobin' as an all-purpose put-down for hundreds of years.

In consequence, Britain was prosperous and free. It is no surprise that the rising powers of Asia should now be seeking to devolve power and responsibility. The tragedy is that Europe, as we shall see, is going in the opposite direction.

It is becoming increasingly clear that 'evolutionary rationalism' is not just the best way to run a government. Since the 1960s, there has been a growing critique of the idea of hierarchy in other fields, too. A substantial corpus of literature, aimed principally at business organisations, elaborates and extends the Hayekian critique. This literature is usually ignored by politicians, but it has a great deal to teach them.

Consider, for example, the research into 'cognitive biases' inspired by Daniel Kahneman and Amos Tversky. Kahneman and Tversky made the discovery that experts are prone to particular kinds of errors of judgement: the sunk costs phenomenon, egocentric distortions, the bandwagon effect and so on. For example, fund managers tend, on average, to underperform the stock exchange: most of us would be better off buying shares at random than asking a professional to do it for us. If professional money men are surprisingly bad at handling our affairs, logic suggests that the same is even truer of the civil servants and ministers who lack the fund managers' incentives.

Or consider 'transactions-cost economics', inspired by the Nobel prize-winning economist Ronald Coase and developed by Oliver Williamson. Williamson's interest was in comparing the costs of running something internally with those of the external market. Among other things, he found that the larger an organisation becomes, and the more it takes on, the less efficient it becomes. Most management consultants know this, of course; but the logic is rarely extended to government departments.

One reason why big organisations become inefficient is communication failure. Subordinates are often reluctant to present the full picture to their line managers, sometimes not wanting to pester their superiors, sometimes wanting to look as if they are able to handle things, sometimes simply being reluctant to be the bearers of bad news. In consequence, line managers can have a *less* complete picture of what is happening than those beneath them. And those at the very top can be the most cut-off of all. As Kenneth Boulding put it: 'The larger and more authoritarian the organisation, the better the chance that its top decision-makers will be operating in purely imaginary worlds.'

Those words have been elaborated and developed in recent management literature, such as *The Myth of Leadership* by Jeffrey Nielsen and *The End of Management* by Kenneth Cloke and Joan Goldsmith. These books and others offer a defiant critique of the traditional notion of leadership. The more hierarchical an organisation, they contend, the less original and flexible it will be.

Most businesses have taken this thinking to heart: top-down command structures are out, internal markets are in. The chief executive of Tesco likes to boast that no more than six levels of hierarchy separate him from the check-out girl. But government ministries remain wholly unreconstructed. How many levels of hierarchy separate the schools minister from the classroom assistant?

Seen in this wider context, top-down politics seems intellectually as well as morally indefensible. It is not simply a denial of freedom, but a denial, too, of technological progress. Yet the administrative class, not just in Britain but across the EU, is indeed in denial. Politicians continue to assert, against all the evidence, that big is beautiful.

Small state advantage

One of the arguments advanced in favour of European integration, for example, is that large blocs are richer and more secure than small nations. But if this were so, China would be wealthier than Hong Kong,

Indonesia than Brunei, France than Monaco – and for that matter, the EU than Switzerland. In fact, the four tiny states that comprise the European Free Trade Association (Switzerland, population 7.6 million; Norway, population 4.8 million; Iceland, population 320,000; Liechtenstein, population 35,000) enjoy a per capita GDP 214 per cent of the EU's: their peoples, in other words, are more than twice as rich as EU citizens.

Confronted by the evidence that many of the world's richest territories are micro-states, our first reaction is often to dismiss them as tax havens. But this is a circular argument. The reason that tiny states became tax havens is because they already had low taxes. And why did they have low taxes? Because they enjoyed the small-state advantages of efficiency and proximity. Their civil services were manageable. There was little opportunity for duplication or waste. Errors were harder to hide, and easier to rectify. Laws designed for small and homogenous populations tended to have fewer unforeseen consequences.

At the same time, decision-makers are more easily held to account in small polities. The journey from conception to actualisation is shorter. There are fewer statutory consultation periods, fewer judicial reviews, fewer civil servants to blunt their ministers' desires. And the ministers themselves are known to their populations. They cannot easily evade responsibility for unpopular decisions by blaming other layers of government or taking refuge in procedural complexity.

It is for these reasons that nine of the ten wealthiest states in the world have populations of less than nine million. The big exception – in both senses of the word – is the United States. But the US proves the rule: it governs itself like a confederation of statelets, vesting key powers in its states and even in its counties.

Many of the peculiar features of American democracy – the election of public officials, from the school board to the Sheriff; the fiscal and legislative autonomy of the 50 states; the use of open primaries to select candidates; term limits and recall procedures to control politicians; open congressional hearings for big appointments; local and state-wide referendums – are designed to prevent law-makers from becoming remote.

Founded in a popular revolt against an autocratic government, the US sought to base its government on what we may loosely call Jeffersonian principles: the notion that decisions should be taken as closely as possible to the people they affect. These principles were intended to keep the people free; but they have served equally to make them prosperous. We shall look in detail at whether and how they might be adapted to British conditions later on. For now, we simply note that a large, complex, pluralist nation can acquire small-state advantages provided it arranges its political system on the basis of decentralisation and maximum accountability.

Analogue politics in a digital age

Never has the expectations gap been so wide. When we book a holiday or buy a DVD we expect choice and immediacy. We browse the internet for options, we click a couple of buttons, and we get what we came for. Compare this to the experience of applying for a driving licence, or getting planning permission – let alone trying to get a child into a particular school.

The technological advances of the past decade have empowered consumers in everything except their dealings with the state. Previous generations were much readier to accept that what they wanted might not be available and that, even when it was, they would have to queue for it. But the internet has created almost unlimited capacity, eliminating storage costs and reducing barriers to entry. Whatever we want, the chances are that someone somewhere will be selling it. And it is now more feasible than ever to deal with that someone – unless that someone is a government agency.

The mismatch between state and private sectors is not a new phenomenon: the free market has always tended, on average, to deliver more efficient outcomes than government departments – a fact that, for at least the past 40 years, has been recognised by most economists. What is new, though, is the extent of the disparity.

In his book *The Long Tail*, Chris Anderson, editor-in-chief of *Wired* magazine, explains how the internet pulverises monoliths. He begins with the examples of music and films. Until now, these industries were driven by the search for blockbusters. A new product had to attract a large number of purchasers in order to recoup its costs. A video, for example, needed to be rented with a certain frequency in order to justify the cost of the shelf space. But the internet has abolished the need for shelf space. A film might be purchased online by only a handful of people; yet it still makes sense to offer the service, since doing so is effectively free. That is the 'long tail' of the title: all the ones and twos that are individually insignificant but that, collectively, represent considerable profit.

From a consumer's point of view, the tail represents a hitherto unimaginable extension of choice. A generation ago, teenagers listened to the music played by a handful of radio stations and watched whatever films were screened by their local cinema. Today, they have Amazon and iTunes and Rhapsody and Netflix and LoveFilm. Not only can they choose what they want, they can increasingly *make* what they want – for another aspect of the long tail is that it breaks down the distinction between amateurs and professionals.

The future is in your hands

Consider, as an example of the phenomenon, the book you are now reading. Until a couple of years ago, the authors would have had two choices: either to find a mainstream publisher willing to take on the project, or to print it themselves.

The latter option would have required an initial investment of perhaps £10,000, including cover artwork, an initial print run and a launch. The books would then sit around in large boxes crowding the authors' homes and offices. And how to sell them? Either by carting them around booksellers in small numbers or, more realistically, by advertising their sale by post, thereby incurring large additional costs.

Since few authors have the resources to do all this, they are effectively obliged to go through a publishing house. And, while publishers obviously want to print popular books, they are not always able to judge what will be popular. Indeed, their business plans are based on the assumption that most of their publications will make a loss, but that this loss will be compensated by the occasional blockbuster. They are, in other words, trying to second-guess the market. Inevitably, mistakes are made: turkeys are commissioned, potentially profitable books refused.

Now, though, there is no need for such mistakes. The internet allows us to publish and advertise our own books. While there will always be room for publicity campaigns, a book can now become successful through word of mouth in a way that would very recently have been inconceivable.

This book is part of a trend which is already transforming the world of publishing. Until you ordered it, it had not been printed. It was stored virtually, waiting for your order.

Publishing books on demand is inventory-free. There are no storage costs. The book can be retailed through conventional distribution channels or direct to retailers via Amazon.com, at a fraction of the cost. It is thus possible to print books for both niche and mass markets without the risks associated with predictive printing and distribution. There is no longer the mass pulping of unsold print runs.

While we hope that many thousands buy this book and read it, it would pay if even only a few hundred people did so. It was inconceivable, even a few months ago, that a book that sold only a few hundred could pay its way.

No longer do publishers have to try to gauge their readers' taste. No longer do authors have to rely on getting their manuscript approved by someone whose sense of what will sell may be imperfect. No longer are readers obliged to choose only from the narrow range offered to them by the professionals. Publishing, in short, has been disintermediated: there is now a more perfect connection between authors and readers. The unlikeliest topics can turn out to have huge markets. Books stand or fall on the basis of demand rather than the whim of a badly-paid manuscript reader. Writers with something interesting to say can outperform even the best established authors.

Wiki-politics

Something similar may be about to happen in the world of politics. Wraith-like, we can see it taking form in the United States, where internet penetration of politics goes deepest. The web has made it possible, as never before, for a politician to come from outside, appealing directly to voters over the heads of party bigwigs. The phenomenon began with Howard Dean, a candidate for the Democratic nomination in 2004. Dean, who based his appeal on an angry and populist opposition to the Iraq war, was heartily disliked by most senior Democrats. Lacking the support of a party machine and of the big financial donors, he looked like being one of the many minnows who contest the early primaries before dropping out. But something surprising happened: the internet allowed him to mobilise a nationwide regiment of foot soldiers and small donors.

Dean ran his party close, but in the end came second. Not so the new-boy senator Barack Obama in 2008. Less of an outsider than Dean, Obama was nonetheless written off before the primaries began. The Clinton family's hold on party structures, and Hillary Clinton's financial muscle, conventional wisdom held, would be insuperable. In the event, Obama managed to raise millions in small donations, appealing directly to the electorate outside the Democratic Party. That appeal – or, rather, Obama's ability to realise his appeal through modern communications – was the basis of his victory in the Democratic primary.

Nothing, though, compares with the phenomenon of Ron Paul, the ultra-libertarian Republican who, on 16 December 2007, broke all records by raising over $6 million from 37,000 online donors *in a single day*. According to Washington insiders, pundits and – most of all – other Republicans, Paul was a maverick almost to the point of lunacy. The only Republican to have opposed the Iraq war, Paul wanted to close down most of the federal government, including the FBI and CIA and the federal tax system. Asked on television what he would have done about the September 11 attacks, he replied that the attacks had succeeded because the federal government was in charge of airline security. If the carriers and their passengers had been responsible for their own safety, he argued, the terrorists would have been thwarted.

Plainly Ron Paul was never going to become President. But he is perhaps the first example of a politician whose appeal was created online. Not only did he outperform his rivals in internet donations; he also tended to come top in online polls. Although his views were not shared by most voters, they turned out not to be quite as off-centre as the pundits assumed. To put it another way, a small group of political professionals – columnists, big donors, party grandees – no longer decides who is mainstream and who is eccentric.

The internet has remade entire industries: record labels, travel agencies, newspapers. But politicians have been much slower to adapt. As Rob Colvile argued in his Centre for Policy Studies pamphlet *Politics, Policy and the Internet*, the political parties tried to fit the internet into their established structures, using it as simply one more tool to get their message across, and often not even doing that terribly well. As Colvile notes, the websites of the main British parties are surprisingly static, in form and content. The only one to attract significant traffic is that of the British National Party, which, never having assembled the clanking machinery of the pre-web era, had fewer habits to set aside. The BNP, for all its Luddite views, is therefore like a country that can move directly from agriculture to services without having to go through de-industrialisation.

Unlearning old ways is painful. Most politicians grew up in an age where whatever a minister announced was intrinsically newsworthy. The very fact of holding ministerial office guaranteed the attention of the handful of political correspondents who controlled the news monopoly. Not any more. Today, politics is reported and disseminated by hundreds of bloggers and amateurs. While lobby correspondents still exist and draw salaries and file copy, they no longer get a page to themselves as they did 15 years ago. A politician must now compel attention by virtue of what he is saying, rather than the position he occupies.

One aspect of this phenomenon, to which, again, many politicians have been slow to adapt, is that parties can no longer deliver 'their' voters. This is most clearly evinced in referendums on European integration. In country after country, the 'Yes' campaigns have begun confidently. After all, they say, all the parties are in favour of closer union. So are all the newspapers. Just as the parties will get their supporters out, runs the reasoning, so the editors will deliver their readers.

In the event, it almost never happens. Every French newspaper and every French party supported the European Constitution in 2004. But 'les bloggeurs' were against and, able as never before to disseminate their case, they won by 55 to 45 per cent. In Ireland in 2008, every newspaper again supported the Constitution (now renamed the Lisbon Treaty), as did every party except Sinn Fein. Once more, there was a lively debate on the internet, which was dominated by 'No' voters; and, once more, the 'No' campaign won.

To put it starkly, the political party as an organism – a complex structure bringing together local branches, clubs, activists, sympathetic newspapers, professions, trade unions, churches and pressure groups – is dying. The modern political party will be protean: a series of *ad hoc*, issue-by-issue coalitions.

Curiously enough, one of the very few politicians to foresee the magnitude of the internet in the mid-1990s was Newt Gingrich, of whom more later. At the time, his tendency to bang on about the web was regarded as a sure sign of eccentricity and unsuitability for office. The politics of his era punished those who were right before their time, favouring instead the cautious men, the careful men, the men who waited until everyone else had spoken before expressing their view. But the present era places a premium on quick reactions. That, too, will eventually impact on the political system.

Why experts get things wrong

One of the most depressing features of contemporary politics is the fetishisation of the 'expert'. The easiest way for a politician on *Question Time* or *Any Questions* to guarantee himself a round of applause is to say, about virtually any subject, 'This is too important to be a political football,' or 'We should leave the professionals to get on with their jobs.'

Everyone likes the idea of the 'expert': the disinterested specialist who can raise his eyes above the partisan scrum and descry the national interest. The trouble is that no such person exists. We all have our prejudices and assumptions, the 'expert' more than most if by 'expert' we mean someone who has spent his entire career in a particular field. To let such an 'expert' invigilate his own profession is a negation of what ought to be the primary purpose of representative government, namely to ensure that state officials are accountable to the taxpayers who indirectly employ them.

'Putting the experts in charge', means, when you think about it, excusing government employees from having to answer directly to the rest of us through our elected tribunes. When Gordon Brown took over as Prime Minister, one of his first announcements was that the NHS would be 'removed from political control'. His statement was a clever and deliberate dog whistle. That phrase has come to mean a coded signal by Right-wing politicians to their supporters on a frequency that won't offend mainstream opinion. But dog whistles can be infra-sound as well as ultra-sound, Left- as well as Right-wing. In promising to remove politicians from the equation, Brown was giving the public sector unions a reassuring wink: 'Don't worry boys: no reforms, no patient power, no performance-related pay.'

Had he put it like that, of course, he would have lost the sympathy of many voters: the NHS has more patients than it has employees. But, by presenting producer-capture as 'letting the professionals get on', he guaranteed himself appreciative murmurs.

What, though, if 'letting the professionals get on' means letting them suit themselves rather than serving the people? What if it means that teachers no longer teach children their letters properly, or that police chiefs become more interested in speed cameras than in catching burglars, or that judges see it as their role always and everywhere to overturn deportation orders? The rest of us then find that we can do nothing about it: a direct consequence of our doltish applause for the politician on *Any Questions* who promised to let the 'experts' get on with things.

Our obsession with 'experts' serves not only to undermine representative democracy, but also, paradoxically, to hamper and constrain the front-line professionals. Top-heavy administration – action days and targets, national curriculums and policing strategies, regional development plans – becomes an end in itself. Civil servants create new agencies and quangos, just as Asimov's robots learned to programme each other without human intervention. A study in May 2008 showed that there are an almost unbelievable 1162 quangos in Britain, costing us £64 billion a year.

We are trapped in a cycle. Every time something goes wrong – a scandal in a care home, the revelation that school meals lack nutritional value – ministers feel the need to 'do something'. That something usually involves a new task force or quango, which then has a vested interest in enlarging its remit and prolonging its existence. Accordingly, it spools out new guidelines and regulations and recommendations and surveys, snarling up the system in more paperwork and almost invariably worsening the situation, which of course leads to calls for yet more intervention and standardisation.

In theory, it is easy enough to identify the solution: devolve responsibility to the lowest possible level and make the decision-makers directly accountable. Or, to put it another way, shift power from Brussels to Westminster, from Whitehall to town halls, from the state to the citizen. Make decisions as closely as possible to the people they affect.

The trouble is that, as things stand, no one has an incentive to make such changes. An engorged and largely self-regulating bureaucracy has grown up whose chief purpose is its own survival. The feebleness of elected representatives in the face of the standing *apparat*, parodied three decades ago in the BBC series *Yes, Minister*, has become even more crippling as politicians have fallen in public esteem, and so have felt obliged to delegate even more powers. To shake off all the constraints on their sovereignty – not only Sir Humphrey, but the Eurocrats, the human rights judges, the 1162 quangos – would require a single-mindedness rarely evinced by any politician who reaches the top. Far easier to manage the *status quo* than to initiate a revolution – especially when the voters keep insisting that the *status quo* is preferable to full democratisation ('letting the politicians interfere').

Politicians cannot change that perception on their own. But there are grounds to hope that it might change despite them. Once again, that hope comes from technological change. The internet, as Chris Anderson notes, breaks down the distinction between amateurs and professionals. One example he gives is that of astronomy, where the distribution of amateur sky-watchers across the world's surface is a resource that no dedicated astronomical centre could match. The freelance sky-watchers are no longer strictly speaking amateurs, but what he calls Pro-Ams.

The think-tank Demos was quick to see the potential political ramifications:

The twentieth century witnessed the rise of professionals in medicine, science, education, and politics. In one field after another, amateurs and their ramshackle organisations were driven out by people who knew what they were doing and had certificates to prove it. The Pro-Am Revolution argues this historic shift is reversing. We're witnessing the flowering of Pro-Am, bottom-up self-organisation and the crude, all or nothing, categories of professional or amateur will need to be rethought.

Indeed so. The internet has given individuals access to the kind of resources and data that, until recently, would have been the property of entire government ministries. This makes it far harder for 'experts' to shelter behind jargon, acronyms and professional cant. Any mother can now download the material necessary to prepare her child for public exams; and, if she does so, she will see that she could convey in less than three hours a day what the school is inculcating in seven. Similarly, anyone with a minor illness can now look up the symptoms and treatment options, effectively replicating what their GP would do.

This is not to say, of course, that we will not need teachers or doctors. Specialisation happens in every system, and it will always make sense to contract out some things to people who concentrate on them. But, as the rigid divisions between 'experts' and everyone else are beginning to crumble, voters will become less tolerant of the idea that professionals should be allowed to run their own affairs without democratic supervision.

Radical Right, conservative Left

Who, though, will initiate this revolution? Who will throw up the barricades and storm the palace? None of the mainstream parties has so far displayed anything like the requisite will-to-power. Left-wing politicians tend to be comfortable with the existing set-up, because they have grasped that the functionaries who run Britain usually default to Left-wing assumptions. It is almost inevitable that a taxpayer-funded bureaucracy will favour higher taxes and more spending. Public bodies and quangos tend to enshrine a set of values – about inclusiveness, accessibility, anti-elitism, corporatism, positive rights – that might well be rejected at the ballot box. Politicians of the Left have understandably reached the view that the power of the standing officials, especially at local level, is a prophylactic against what they see as the populism of Right-wing administrations.

So why do Right-wing politicians put up with it? Precisely because they tend to be small-c conservatives. The desire to work within the system rather than to change it is encoded deep in their DNA. Their attitude has a respectable intellectual pedigree. Edmund Burke taught his own and subsequent generations that change always involves upheaval and unforeseen consequences, and should therefore be embraced moderately, proportionately and only in response to an identified and remediable problem. To quote the third Viscount Falkland: 'When it is not necessary to change, it is necessary not to change.' Or, as the most conservative of all Tory Prime Ministers, the third Marquess of Salisbury put it: 'If anything happens, it will be for the worse, and it is therefore in our interest that as little should happen as possible.'

These views are faithfully echoed by many Conservative front-benchers today. 'The trouble with these quangos,' they say, 'is not that they are quangos, but that they're stuffed with Lefties. It'll be a different story when our people are in charge.' Or: 'The trouble with schools is that teachers are doing the wrong thing: when we take over, we'll make sure they have more power to impose discipline, and teach decent British history, and use synthetic phonics so that children learn to read properly.' Or: 'The trouble with Regional Development Agencies is that they contain too many trade unionists and not enough business people.'

This is fundamentally to misunderstand the nature of the standing bureaucracy and the quango state. A Tory councillor on the local health authority, or a businessman on the Regional Development Agency, will usually absorb osmotically the assumptions of his colleagues and seek to aggrandise the power of the body on which he happens to sit. Even if he does not, he will be safely outnumbered by those who see a greater role for their agency as an end in itself.

Having for centuries defended an essentially conservative settlement, Tories find it hard to adjust to their present powerlessness. The same arguments that were used to defend an Establishment made up of bishops and generals and hanging judges are now being trotted out in favour of the new Establishment: an Establishment of human rights lawyers, BBC executives, equality commissioners and Eurocrats. 'If it ain't broke, don't fix it' is perhaps the quintessential Tory belief. But what when it is broke?

Historically, it was the Left that sought to disperse power among the people. This high-minded aim informed and elevated the English radical tradition over the centuries. It was the cause of the Levellers and the Chartists and the Suffragettes, the cause of religious toleration and meritocracy, of the secret ballot and universal education. The Left is right to take immense pride in these achievements, which almost no one now questions.

These days, though, the radical cause should have different targets. The elites have altered in character and composition. The citizen is far less likely to be impacted by the decisions of dukes or bishops than by those of NICE or his local Local Education Authority. The employees of these and similar agencies are, today, the unaccountable Crown office-holders against whom earlier generations of radicals would have railed.

Yet, with some exceptions – among whom, in a place of special honour, stands Tony Benn – few contemporary British Leftists show any interest in dispersing power when doing so would mean challenging public sector monopolies. The Left, in short, has let the standard of radicalism slide from its fingers. The question is whether the Right will snatch it up.

A lesson from America

The Tories spent most of the twentieth century in office, and were not especially interested in diffusing the powers of government. Under Salisbury, they opposed the very introduction of elected local councils; and, within recent memory, they were the party of rate-capping, of the abolition of the GLC, of the uniform business rate. To this day, the Conservatives are seen as the party of the Establishment: the party of public schools and London clubs and black-tie dinners.

Their condition, however, is not incurable. The US Republicans once had an analogous disadvantage. In the middle years of the twentieth century, the GOP was seen in many quarters as the political arm of old money and big business. It had the odd populist, of course, such as the foul-mouthed Senator Joe McCarthy. But it seemed to be removed from the aspirations of the majority, in personnel, policy and presentation. It was in almost structural opposition in Congress, and tended to win the White House only when it fielded non-partisan candidates.

In their seminal study, *The Right Nation*, John Micklethwait and Adrian Wooldridge chronicle the transformation of the Republicans from an East Coast, preppy, country club party that kept losing into a Sun-Belt, demotic, anti-Washington party that keeps winning. The Republicans have come back in both Houses and in gubernatorial contests, and have won seven out of the past ten presidential elections.

The Republicans did not win on their own. As Micklethwait and Wooldridge emphasise, they were part of a wider conservative movement. Around the party was a nexus of friendly organisations: gun clubs, radio stations, home-school associations, evangelical churches. These bodies do not have obvious counterparts in Britain, a difference which places the Conservative Party in the awkward position of being expected both to stimulate public demand for its ideas and then to position itself as the beneficiary of that demand.

Britain has the odd Tory-friendly pressure group, notably the Taxpayers' Alliance, and a well-organised Euro-sceptic movement. But, in general, supposedly neutral lobby institutions, from Liberty to Age Concern, from Oxfam to the Child Poverty Action Group, come from the Left. It is fair to point out, too, that the labour movement in the US was never as strong as in Britain, which means that there is less of a tribal vote for the Left among American blue-collar workers. This creates an opening for the Right-wing party to appeal to those voters on what psephologists call 'values' issues.

Nor, in general, are British voters as naturally libertarian as their cousins. You would not see bumper stickers in the United Kingdom proclaiming: 'I love my country, I hate my government.' And, of course, power is dispersed in the US. These are important differences.

Nonetheless, the single most important component in the Republicans' success is something that the British Right could mimic, namely their determination to articulate the electorate's disdain for politicians and functionaries. As we have seen, British voters have become bitterly cynical about their political process – arguably with more cause than Americans. But they cannot find any channel for that cynicism except abstention or voting for a fringe party.

Tapping into anti-politician feeling is, by definition, not an easy task for politicians. It took the GOP a generation, and it involves far more than making speeches about freedom. The Republicans needed to do two related things.

First, they had to stand unequivocally for localism and devolution. It was their espousal of states' rights – in the first instance, opposing the bussing of schoolchildren – that began their revival. Part of this struggle was and remains the battle against judicial activism, which they have managed to turn into a populist cause.

Second, they had to show that they were not simply interested in grasping the levers of power. A series of anti-politics policies, ranging from term limits for legislators to limitations on budgets, helped establish in the public mind that at least some Republicans were with 'us' against 'them' – with, that is, the country against its functionariat.

These things did not do the trick on their own. But they were a necessary condition for the success of the Republicans, as for that of any conservative party. Once the GOP had established itself as being on the side of the people – or, at least, a good many of the people – it earned itself the right to be listened to on other subjects.

Before we turn to the specific legislation by which an incoming British administration might do something similar – that is, fundamentally alter the role and powers of government itself – it is worth looking at the document which stands as an embodiment and instrument of the Republican revival.

The Contract with America

Newt Gingrich is not a name politicians like to invoke these days. His career followed the Powellite script and ended in failure. On the way, however, he achieved something quite extraordinary. He ended 40 years of one-party rule in the House of Representatives. Nor did his victory herald only a brief Republican interlude, as was widely expected at the time: Congress has returned to something approaching two-party alternation.

Even more impressive, however, was his legislative record. Gingrich habituated American voters to an idea that they had almost wholly given up on, namely that politicians can keep their promises.

In 1994, Gingrich made Republican candidates sign up to a short and highly specific document, the Contract with America. Unlike a traditional party manifesto, it was brief, plain and taut, with no wriggle-room and no small print. The full text of the Contract is printed as Appendix One.

At first glance, it seems that a surprising amount of the Contract with America is concerned with the internal reform of Congress and its procedures. But Gingrich had accurately sensed that voters no longer confided in their representatives – that, as in contemporary Britain, they regarded politicians as a breed apart, a smug and self-interested elite. Before doing anything else, he knew that he had to address their criticism. Hence the very first pledge: to make Congress subject to the same laws as the rest of the country.

Most observers regarded this as an abstruse and eccentric commitment. But it turned out to be perhaps the single most popular promise of all. Although the practical consequences were limited – Congress had exempted itself from elements of employment and anti-discrimination law – the political ramifications were enormous. A common criticism of the US Congress in the 1990s, as of our Parliament today, was that its members were 'above the law'. Here, then, was a clear and unequivocal way of answering that criticism.

Further articles promised to reduce the number of staffers, to cut budgets and to make life harder for lobbyists. All these were procedural rather than legislative commitments, dealing with internal House reforms and, again, the pundits concluded that the GOP was making a terrible mistake by focusing on what would be seen as remote and recondite issues. But the voters, who had become contemptuous of politicians as a caste, looked on with sudden interest.

Then came a clear ten-point legislative programme, which was to be delivered within 100 days: a balanced budget law, welfare reform, anti-crime measures and so on (see Appendix One). 'If we don't deliver the Contract, sack us!' said Republican candidates. The columnists dismissed it as a cheap trick that no one would fall for, but the electorate was intrigued and engaged. Voters turned out in large numbers, and with a sense of optimism. The Republicans took office for the first time since Eisenhower's day.

'Now what will you do?' demanded journalists as the results came in.

'Implement the Contract,' Gingrich would reply.

'Come on, now, the campaign is over. What are you *really* going to do?'

'Read this,' the tubby Georgian would say, thrusting a copy of the document into their hands.

Amazingly, he meant it. The internal House reforms were voted through as promised, and nine out of the ten Bills were approved within 100 days (actually, within 96 days, since the Republicans, in keeping with their pro-family stance, were determined to allow Congressmen to spend Passover or Easter with their families). The tenth Bill, proposing term limits for legislators, needed a two-thirds majority, and was blocked on the floor.

Only now, perhaps, do we have the sense of distance needed to perceive the magnitude of what happened in the mid-1990s. The Contract with America did not simply mark the comeback of the Republicans in a legislature that was thought to belong to the Democratic Party. Far more important, it initiated a wholly new approach to politics.

Rather than promising to do better, the Republicans promised to do *less*. Rather than offering competence, experience or managerialism, they promised – and delivered – an anti-politician revolution. In doing so, they did not simply restore the standing of their party; they restored, at least in some measure, the reputation of their legislature.

They did not promise the earth. They eschewed the hackneyed phrases that so often make up the politicians' idiom. They made simple, unequivocal pledges that clearly established them as being on the side of the people, not the system.

Could something similar happen in Britain? Could we restore honour and meaning and optimism to the electoral process? Could we disperse power from remote elites to local representatives? Of course we could. But, as in the US, we must begin by tackling people's cynicism about their entire political class; and that will require an overhaul of Parliament proportionate to the public's contempt.

Part Two

Twelve months to renew Britain

In his book *The Other Invisible Hand*, Julian Le Grand, Tony Blair's former ideologue and adviser, argued that Labour had gone through three phases in its approach to public services: trusting the professionals; not trusting the professionals (that is, imposing targets and management structures on them); and consulting the consumers.

Phase one was characteristic of the early Blair years, as it had been of the Major years. It is, as we have seen, the facile choice, the choice of the politician eager for cheap applause, and is characterised by allowing state employees (or 'front-line professionals' as politicians invariably call them in this context) to set their own budgets and targets. The result, inescapably, is that budgets increase but productivity does not, leading to public anger.

To address this anger, politicians then shift to phase two: performance management. No longer trusting the professionals, government starts laying down what they ought to do. Targets, as we have seen, tend to have unintended consequences – and, all too often, to fail in their intended consequences, too. In Christopher Booker's memorable phrase, they use a sledgehammer to miss a nut.

Hence phase three: a voice for consumers. Eventually convinced that producers will always, if unconsciously, put their own interests first, the late Blair government attempted to ensure representation for consumers through, for example, patient forums to make sure the NHS was locally accountable. But, of course, giving consumers a voice is not the same as empowering them.

The frustration was visible in Blair's speeches and, even more, in his unscripted comments. He lumped in the public sector unions with the 'forces of conservatism', spoke of bearing 'scars on my back' from his attempts to overhaul the system and, at the end, in a moment of demob candour, admitted that every time he had attempted reform, he wished in retrospect that he had gone further.

The challenge for a new government is to learn from Blair's experience rather than wasting a decade and tens of billions of pounds reaching the point that he reached at the fag-end of his administration. It is vital that the next government learn from its predecessor's mistakes – in other words, that it move directly to phase four: choice, whether as a consumer or as a voter.

This book is intended to facilitate that process. Having explained why the state is malfunctioning, we now set out in some detail what a new government needs to do to repair it. Not only do we posit what should be done; we also suggest how to do it, setting out the requisite legal acts. We propose a 12-month legislative programme which, if followed, would result in a revolution. That word is much overused, but what follows is nothing less than a turning of the wheel, a righting of that which has been placed on its head. At present, many citizens feel that they are working for the state; we aim to make the state serve its citizens.

Everything that follows is premised on three principles:

- Decisions should be taken as closely as possible to the people who are affected by them
- Decision-makers should be directly accountable
- The citizen should be as free as possible from state coercion.

In many cases, devolution to the lowest possible level will mean to the individual. But there are plainly areas of policy which require an element of collective endeavour: policing, for example. In such areas, there should be maximum accountability and proximity. Thus, in the case of policing, as we shall see, we propose placing our constabularies under directly elected Sheriffs.

A handful of policy areas are, by their nature, national: defence, immigration, foreign policy. Although it is not practicable to localise policy in these areas, it *is* possible to democratise it – through, for example, parliamentary control over ambassadorial appointments and treaty ratifications, annual quotas for immigration and radical changes in defence procurement policy.

The first lines of such a manifesto appeared shortly after the 2005 general election in a publication called *Direct Democracy: An Agenda for a New Model Party*, co-authored by 22 Conservative MPs, MEPs, MSPs and activists. The programme was serialised in *The Daily Telegraph* and the ideology which informed it became known as localism, and was soon endorsed by a majority of the 2005 Conservative intake (the full list of supporters appears as Appendix Two).

Localism went from novelty to orthodoxy with almost no intervening stage. Within days, four of the five declared Conservative leadership contenders had endorsed the idea. (The fifth was Ken Clarke, who magisterially flicked two nicotine-stained fingers at us, scoffing that the only country to approximate our ideal was Switzerland, and that no one he knew could name a single Swiss politician.)

Once he had been elected as Conservative leader, David Cameron declared: 'I passionately believe we need to localise power, as recommended by the Direct Democracy movement of Conservative activists and MPs.' He went on to commit a future Tory government to the democratisation of policing and to the break-up of the patronage powers enjoyed by the Prime Minister under Crown prerogative.

Soon, the other parties were joining in. David Miliband, Alan Milburn, Nick Clegg and even, however implausibly, Gordon Brown, began to talk about empowering communities, about decentralising power, about localism. As is the way of these things, many politicians were simply using a catchy new buzzword to mean whatever they happened to have believed all along. There was a danger that localism would become so vague a term as to be meaningless.

Accordingly, in the summer of 2007, we produced *The Localist Papers*, published by the Centre for Policy Studies and again serialised in *The Daily Telegraph*, six pamphlets setting out how the principles of localism might apply to specific policy areas.

This book draws on some of these ideas, extends and elaborates them, and examines how they could form the legislative programme of an incoming government. We have grouped them under ten headings: cleaning up Westminster; restoring confidence in the criminal justice system; making Parliament sovereign; empowering parents; returning power to local government; empowering patients; shifting people from welfare to work; repealing unwanted laws; forging a British foreign policy; and adopting direct democracy.

At the end, we indicate the steps that an incoming government would need to take, whether in the form of an Order in Council, a Motion of the House (to effect reform of the Commons itself) or a Bill. Such a programme could be completed in just under seven months. Allowing for other urgent business and unforeseen exigencies, as well as recesses, we believe it could be delivered within a single year's parliamentary session. There might be a need for a spillover session, even for some legislation on Fridays. But, after those 12 months, the powers and status of Parliament would be altered forever.

What is being proposed is not a recalibration of the state, but a redefinition; not a promise to do better, but a promise to do entirely different things. Our aim is nothing less than the restoration of liberty to the individual, dignity to the legislature and purpose to the ballot box.

We begin with Parliament itself. Until they recover public confidence, MPs will not have the moral authority to begin a task of such magnitude. Before putting the affairs of the nation in order, parliamentarians must order their own house. And that means undertaking reforms commensurate with the extent of public anger.

1. Cleaning up Westminster

- ➤ Abolition of MPs' perks
- ➤ Transparency for remaining expenses
- ➤ MPs bound by the same laws as everyone else
- ➤ Election of the Speaker by secret ballot
- ➤ Election of committee chairmen and parliamentary officials
- ➤ Committee hearings for senior civil servants and heads of executive agencies
- ➤ Annualised budgets for each department and agency
- ➤ Scrapping state funding for parties and transparency in donations
- ➤ A smaller ministerial payroll
- ➤ A smaller House of Commons
- ➤ Open primaries
- ➤ Lords reform

It is no coincidence that the Contract with America began with internal reforms to Congress. There was a strong sense in the US then, as there is in Britain now, that legislators had lost their moral authority, that they should earn their constituents' confidence before attempting anything else.

There is a sense of anger and contempt for MPs in Britain without recorded precedent. Superficially, it is focused on MPs' expenses; but there is more to it than that. MPs, after all, are no more venal than in the past. The difference is that, these days, MPs have disencumbered themselves of meaningful power. Unable to effect change in their constituents' lives, they are seen as freeloading. And so, suddenly, every expense claim they make is resented.

A deep-clean of parliamentary expenses is a necessary start to restoring voters' trust in their representatives; but it is only a start. If MPs want to recover the respect of their constituents, they must also recover their sovereignty.

Expenses reform

Worse than the row over parliamentary allowances was the way in which some MPs responded to public criticism. The Speaker, Michael Martin, behaved like a touchy and stubborn shop steward, opposing all reform on principle.

When the pressure for change became irresistible, the Speaker set up something called the Members' Estimates Committee, a dozen grandees with 136 years of service among them and with constituency majorities of nearly 9,000 each. These MPs felt secure enough to oppose full transparency and at the same time recommend maintaining a version of the most controversial of the allowances: the so-called 'John Lewis list', which allowed MPs to pay mortgages, improve their homes and purchase furniture at public expense. Instead of claiming for individual items, the committee urged that MPs be given an additional tax-free grant of over £4,000 a year.

When the vote eventually came, MPs rejected the proposal to scrap the John Lewis list (although they limited the proportion that could be spent on household goods) and, far more bizarrely, rejected not only the publication of their expenses, but even the auditing of them.

Things have now reached the point where the only reform proportionate to public anger is to scrap all parliamentary allowances except the costs of running a constituency office and travelling between Westminster and the constituency, and to require these last two to be made public.

Citizen legislators

In the longer term, though, we need to consider whether the current system – a full-time Parliament with full-time MPs – is the most appropriate one. The professionalisation of politics has been accompanied by a growing disdain for politicians, based on the sense that they are a breed apart.

If the agenda set out in this book were implemented in full, several of the policies that now concern MPs would be devolved to local government. Although Parliament would gain some powers – from judges, from quangos and, above all, from the EU – it would cease to control a good deal of domestic policy: policing and welfare would become the province of our counties and cities, while education and healthcare would require far less day-to-day administration than at present. MPs would no longer be expected to function as social workers within their constituencies, but would be freer to focus on larger national and international issues.

In such circumstances, it might be worth considering the model favoured in Switzerland and in several US states, where the legislatures meet for only a few days each year, and where parliamentarians are compensated for their time, but are not given a substantial salary, and are instead expected to continue with whatever trade or profession they had prior to their election.

The same rules for everyone
Nothing vindicates the sense that MPs are a class apart as much as their ability to exempt themselves from the rules that they apply to the rest of the country. To take some examples:

- When the law on sex discrimination was invoked to challenge Labour's imposition of all-women shortlists, MPs concluded (correctly) that this was not what the Act had been intended for. But instead of repealing the Act, they amended it to exclude political parties from its provisions – an option not open to the many other employers who have suffered from its misapplication.
- When the Freedom of Information Act was invoked to secure the disclosure of MPs' expenses claims, an amendment was moved to exclude Parliament from its provisions.
- While the Labour Government was imposing a massive tax on private pensions, MPs were voting to make their own pensions still more generous.
- Smoking is now banned in public places. But Parliament waived the rules with reference to its own bars.

These issues may not be of the magnitude of some addressed in this book. But, in order to gain the right to be listened to on other subjects, MPs must first demonstrate their good faith to a public that has ceased to give them the benefit of the doubt. They need to convince a sceptical electorate that they are not members of a separate caste, but citizens who have assumed a specific and limited job, namely ensuring that the organs of the state are held to account.

Other than the one specific privilege which MPs have always exercised – that of being able to speak freely in Parliament without the threat of a libel suit (a privilege which applies only within the Chamber itself) – no special rights should attach to being a parliamentarian. An MP is an ordinary citizen, there to represent his fellows. The moment he ceases to look like one, he loses his moral mandate.

Elect the Speaker and committee chairmen

It is not widely appreciated that the Speaker is not elected in a free and fair ballot. A quirk of procedure means that one candidate is proposed in a parliamentary motion, and all the other candidates are put forward as amendments to that motion. If there are only two candidates, the system is impartial; but if there are any more, it gives a huge advantage to the original nominee since, unless one of his rivals wins an outright majority, his will be the last name in the frame, and voting against him at that stage would nullify the entire procedure. Because the government decides whose name is on the original motion, it can effectively rig the process for its favourite candidate.

Last time, Michael Martin's name was the one moved and, sure enough, he won comfortably. Ever since, there have been complaints that he has favoured the Government, as much against its own backbenchers as against the Opposition parties. One especially outrageous example was his decision to disallow, on no obvious grounds, an amendment by Labour Euro-sceptics calling for a referendum on the Lisbon Treaty.

The Speaker should be the supreme guarantor and exemplar of parliamentary supremacy. He ought to embody the independence and the dignity of the House of Commons. When he is supine before the executive, Parliament as a whole is diminished.

A Speaker genuinely elected by Parliament by secret ballot might be readier to defend the House *vis-à-vis* the Government. As well as chiding MPs who ask impertinent or unparliamentary questions of ministers, he might occasionally intervene the other way around, ordering ministers to answer questions properly.

The same applies to committee chairmen. At present, they are to all intents and purposes appointed by the Whips, who get together to decide the composition of the committees. A secret ballot of the whole House would give them an independent mandate.

Finally, senior parliamentary officers – the Serjeant-at-Arms, the Clerk of the House of Commons – should be approved by Parliament itself.

Parliamentary hearings

The most important way to reverse the shift in power from the legislature to the executive is through the power of appointments: the original demand of the Parliamentary side in the English Civil War.

Through an accident of history, the Prime Minister has inherited more or less intact the powers that once attached to the monarch: the award of peerages, decorations and ecclesiastical livings, treaty-making powers and, much the most important, the power to appoint officials to the mass of executive agencies that we loosely call quangos.

These powers should pass to Parliament. Heads of executive agencies should be appointed following open hearings, and should have to come back and make the case annually for a renewal of their budgets.

No state funding

If political parties need money, they should have to ask for it politely, not compel it by force of law. A ban on the state funding of political activity would mean the phasing out of 'Short money' (the resources given to all Opposition parties in the Commons) and of the generous Communications Allowance, which allows MPs to promote themselves in their constituencies at public expense. It would also mean the end of hidden donations, including election broadcasts and the free postage of election addresses. At the same time, donations over £1,000 should be made public.

We have already seen how the internet has transformed political donations in the US, shifting the balance from a small number of massive contributors to millions of online donors typically giving less than $100 each. There is no reason that the same thing should not happen in Britain. But, if it didn't, parties would simply have to get by with less.

Fewer MPs, fewer ministers

We should look seriously at a statutory limitation on the number of days that Parliament sits: few things are as deleterious to the public weal as under-employed legislators. In the same vein, we should substantially reduce the number of MPs. The US House of Representatives administers a population nearly six times that of the United Kingdom with only 435 members.

We should set an upper limit to the number of ministers. A swollen payroll vote not only enlarges the executive at the expense of Parliament: it also leads to unnecessary legislation, as each new appointment creates a new portfolio, and each new minister seeks to justify his salary.

Nor is there a need for every minister within this reduced total to be an MP. The Prime Minister should be free to appoint non-MPs as ministers (without the farce of ennobling them), provided their appointment is approved by the relevant parliamentary committee in an open hearing.

Taken together with the other steps we have proposed, this reform should tackle what is perhaps the most serious cause of Parliament's feebleness: the desire of every backbencher to become a frontbencher. As long as most MPs want to be ministers, Parliament will be a creature of the majority Whips, and will therefore fail in its chief function, namely to hold the Government to account. As well as creating fewer opportunities for ministerial advancement, we should create more opportunities for parliamentary advancement, so that it again becomes possible to have an honourable career as a parliamentarian, without aspiring to ministerial office.

Open primaries

Most MPs' failings can be explained by a single fact: 70 per cent of constituencies in Britain are the property of a single party. Once in, provided they do not fall out with their local activists, most MPs are effectively irremovable.

This knowledge, naturally enough, skews their loyalty towards their party rather than their constituents. At the same time, it shields them from the consequences of their actions. An MP in a safe seat can vote against the interests of his constituents with something close to impunity. What he cannot afford to do is vote against his Whips to the point where he loses the right to stand in his party's interest.

Proportional representation would make the problem even worse: a party list system concentrates yet more power in the hands of the Whips.

The best solution to the problem is to give local people a say in who should be the main parties' candidates. Then, instead of feeling that they were being presented with a *fait accompli*, people would have the opportunity, early on, to identify 'their' candidate: the candidate in whose success they felt they had a stake. The British public responded with more interest and enthusiasm to the 2008 US primaries than to political developments within this country. That should tell us something.

Primaries developed in the US as a way to keep the parties in touch with the electorate. The American voting system, like the British, is majoritarian, which tends to favour a two-party polity. But in the US, as in Britain, the two parties were not always the same: a progression of Federalists, Whigs, Know-Nothings and others marched across the stage before the current duopoly. What anchored the Republicans and Democrats in place? Open primaries, which ensured that the existing parties adapted to new trends rather than being displaced as a result of them.

Above all, open primaries prevented safe districts from becoming politically stagnant. In the years after Reconstruction, most of the old Confederacy was a one-party system in a way unknown in Britain. The Tories have occasionally lost seats in Surrey. Labour sometimes loses seats in Glasgow. But the Democrats never came close to losing the South. This did not mean, however, that their Congressmen could relax. They knew that if they developed a reputation for having gone native in Washington, or if they voted too often against their districts, they would be challenged for the Democratic nomination. Think, for a moment, of how open primaries would concentrate the minds of British MPs in safe seats.

No one, of course, can tell a political party how to select its candidates. But the likelihood is that if one of the major parties adopted open primaries, the others would feel obliged to follow.

We should therefore legislate to ensure that a party has the right to ask local authorities to conduct a full ballot on its behalf (with the party meeting the costs). Whether parties chose to avail themselves of this entitlement would be up to them.

The House of Lords
Altering the function or composition of the House of Lords is not something to be attempted within the first year, for one reason above all: a

prolonged battle on this issue would almost certainly make it impossible to deliver the rest of the agenda on time.

Nonetheless, it is worth stating, if only for the record, that the composition of the House of Lords is impossible to reconcile with the principle of direct democracy. Indeed, a largely appointed chamber is the worst of all imaginable options. The current chamber, whatever the individual qualities of its members, embodies everything that is wrong with the administration of Britain. It is made up of people who can pass laws without having to justify themselves to those who must obey their laws. The appointments system tends to throw up atypical candidates – if not ex-politicians, then often people who have spent their careers in the corporate or representative branch of their professions, rather than the professions themselves. Someone who has worked his way up through the Confederation of British Industry, the Trades Union Congress, the British Medical Association or the National Farmers Union, is likelier to end up on the red benches than a practising businessman, manual worker, doctor or farmer.

At the same time, a directly elected chamber – although plainly an improvement on the *status quo* – would bring yet more under-employed lawmakers into play. An ideal Upper House would reflect the temper of the country as a whole without establishing a new tier of politicians. How to constitute such a chamber merits a longer study than this one but, as an example of what might work, we suggest bringing together a geographically and politically representative selection of existing elected figures. For instance, we could constitute a Senate of seconded county and borough councillors in proportion to their parties' representation in each shire or city, which would meet for three or four days each month, with considerable powers to block or amend legislation, but no power of initiative. As well as correcting the metropolitan bias of the current chamber, this reform would exalt the role of local government which, as we shall see, would be becoming considerably more important in any event. The bestowal of life peerages – or, indeed, hereditary titles – could then devolve to the monarch, ensuring that they became wholly a mark of service, devoid of political significance.

2. A return to law, order and accountability

➢ Police to be placed under directly elected Sheriffs
➢ Sheriffs to control all aspects of local policing, prioritising offences and setting budgets
➢ Sheriffs also to administer probation, young offenders institutes, community service orders and prison places
➢ Sheriffs to take over the role of the Crown Prosecution Service
➢ Sheriffs to set local sentencing guidelines
➢ Directly elected mayors to perform the Sheriff's role where the metropolitan area is congruent with the constabulary (currently only London)

The political discussion about crime is often a numbingly boring argument about statistics. Overall crime recorded by the police seems to have risen (so the Conservatives rely on this statistic) while crime reported by the public seems, until very recently, to have fallen (so Labour relies on that). As far as we can tell, certain classes of crime have fallen, notably burglary and car crime, while others have risen, notably violence and anti-social behaviour.

The truth is that 'overall crime' (rather like overall GDP) is an irrelevance. What matters to people is local crime (or their own wealth). And here, the national trends are worrying. For while everyone must welcome the fall in acquisitive crime against homes and cars (a fall, by the way, which has been achieved more because of private investment in alarm technology rather than because of better policing), it is violence and anti-social behaviour which bothers people most.

Conventional policing – based on evidence and detection – is unable to address the problem of anti-social behaviour which, in its most extreme form, leads to the knife culture that has very suddenly taken hold among teenagers in many cities. This sort of crime is not, like acquisitive crime, a rational, if immoral, professional endeavour that can be reduced by rational professional action by the authorities to alter the balance of risk and reward. The prevalence of low-level disorder and random violence is an inchoate, angry, irrational expression of social collapse.

This collapse is happening both 'internally' and 'externally'. The 'internal' collapse is the decline of healthy families and communities, the informal social networks which sustain decent behaviour among individuals. The 'external' collapse is the decline in the effective enforcement of the law by the agency responsible for it: the police. The two are linked, of course: families and communities suffer when the police do not do their job, and the police's job is made harder when families and communities are not strong.

What the police are for

This essential link was once the founding principle of the police force. 'Police, at all times, should maintain a relationship with the public that gives reality to the historic tradition that the police are the public and the public are the police,' said Sir Robert Peel in his statement of principles with which he established the Metropolitan Police Force in 1829.

Today, there is an increasing amount of lip-service paid to this principle – and a decrease in actual implementation of it. 'Working together for a safer London,' proclaims the Met's new, expensively redesigned logo at Scotland Yard. Yet behind the building's blank façade sit thousands of police officers doing precisely the opposite of 'working together' with the community. They are busy devising new processes to 'connect' with the public, but which in fact alienate them further.

There is no more illustrative example of the modern culture of British policing than the proposal in the Macpherson report – since implemented by this government – that officers should fill in a form every time they stop a member of the public in the street. The pointless bureaucracy involved in this requirement is outrageous enough: it takes up seven minutes of an officer's time per person stopped, and thereby discourages him or her from engaging with the public or stopping suspicious individuals. More fundamental, though, is the assumption behind the requirement. This is that the police's relations with the community need to be monitored from above: that every contact between a police officer and a citizen must be mediated by an official process, so that the police's relations with society can be assessed on the basis of statistical returns. The form already contains a question on the individual's racial group, and it has recently been suggested that the individual's religion might be noted down too. Thus does an initiative intended to improve the police's relations with the London public – particularly ethnic minorities – end up an intrusive and deeply illiberal attempt by the state to monitor the behaviour of its agents and peer into the personal circumstances of British citizens. The police and the public have never been more remote from each other.

How do you sack a Chief Constable?

The attempt to ensure the police and the public 'work together' has been enacted from precisely the wrong direction: from above. Local Strategic Partnerships, Crime and Disorder Reduction Partnerships and Community Safety Plans are just a few of the initiatives designed in Whitehall, implemented locally, to 'connect' the police with other 'stakeholders' in the community. In recent years the Home Secretary has assumed more and more powers over local forces, including the power to appoint and dismiss Chief Constables on a whim – as we saw when David Blunkett, responding to the public furore following the Soham murders, demanded the resignation of the Chief Constable of Norfolk, despite the local Police Authority supporting him.

Police Authorities are supposed to represent the community in the supervision of the police. They are one of the three pillars in the 'tripartite' structure implemented in 1964, the others being the Home Secretary and the Chief Constable. Over the years, and especially since 1997, the Police Authority has become by far the weakest of the pillars. Chief Constables are accountable in practice not to the representatives of the community but to the Home Office in Whitehall, which works to ensure – through targets, central funding streams, and bureaucratic audit and inspections – that local forces implement national policies designed to bring down national crime figures. The Home Office has imposed *de facto* national control of police forces.

If one reason for the impotence of Police Authorities is the encroaching power of the Home Office, another is their own lack of moral authority. Police Authorities are appointed bodies, comprising local councillors (on a party proportional basis), Home Office-appointed 'independent' members, and local magistrates. They are anonymous quangos made up of local worthies who, albeit with the best of intentions, generally see it as their job to support 'their' Chief Constable against attacks on his or her performance. It is widely understood that one of the key roles of a Chief Constable is to 'manage' the local Police Authority; that is, to ensure that no complaint or trouble comes from that quarter.

The 1964 tripartite system has failed to create effective local accountability. Chief Constables obey the Home Office, not the community. Few people know Police Authorities exist – even fewer know who sits on them; they are no longer effective (if they ever were) in establishing local policing priorities. People rightly feel alienated from their local police forces.

The saga of Sir Ian Blair
The total absence of accountability is made flesh in the unfortunate form of the most senior police officer in Britain, Sir Ian Blair. The Met Commissioner has lurched from crisis to crisis. At first, he had strong support from Labour politicians, who approved of his apparent belief that the primary purpose of a police force is not to prevent crime, but to promote anti-racism. Sir Ian was certainly an articulate proponent of this agenda. Indeed, if he had concentrated on doing his job, rather than on telling us what a good job he was doing, he might have avoided a good deal of trouble. His elevation of PR over actual policing was neatly symbolised by the fact that, virtually at the moment that the Tube bombers were detonating their devices, he was telling listeners of the *Today* Programme that his force 'set the gold standard for counter-terrorism'.

After the bombing, he was quick to assure everyone that the atrocity had nothing to do with Islam. A week later, he told us that his officers were going around with 'big grins'.

Then came news that a man had been slain at Stockwell Underground station. Within hours, Sir Ian announced that the shooting had been in connection with the Tube bombing. Then, for several days, while the real Tube bombers remained on the run, stories were circulated about Mr de Menezes having been an illegal immigrant and having jumped the ticket barrier. When Sir Ian was finally forced to admit that his officers had killed the wrong man, he insisted that police action was not 'the underlying cause' of Mr de Menezes's death. *Not the underlying cause?* It is hard to see how else we should describe holding someone down and loosing five bullets into the back of his skull.

Nor was it only Stockwell. The gaffes and blunders went on and on. After two young girls had been murdered in Soham, Sir Ian attacked the press for its 'institutional racism' in overemphasising a crime with white victims, an observation not borne out when the *Guardian* counted the column inches dedicated to black crime victims. Not that this dented the newspaper's support for its champion. According to one of its columnists, the clamour against the Metropolitan Police Commissioner had been whipped up by 'the reactionaries in the force and their friends in the press', who had never forgiven his enthusiasm for the Macpherson reforms.

Outside the *Guardian*, however, Sir Ian was running out of friends. In November 2007, the London Assembly passed a motion of no confidence in him. Sir Ian responded by taunting them with their powerlessness: 'I have stated my position, if you have the power to remove me, go on.' If a classical artist had wanted to use a single tableau to illustrate what was wrong with how contemporary Britain was run, how powers had shifted from elected representatives to permanent functionaries, he could have done no better than to depict that scene.

In July 2008, it emerged that the new London mayor, Boris Johnson, armed with the third largest mandate in Europe after the French and Portuguese presidents, also wanted Sir Ian to go. (There had been further scandals and pratfalls in the intervening months, notably a row about the award of a £3 million contract to one of Sir Ian's friends.) The lawyers made clear that the mayor had no such power. The Met Commissioner, using the last-ditch defence of every quangocrat, protested that this position was in danger of becoming 'politicised'. But senior policemen – Sir Ian more than most – were already advancing a contentious political agenda, not least in their active lobbying for internment powers and other anti-terrorist legislation. The question is not whether the people running the police should be *political* – something they can hardly avoid – but whether they should be *elected*.

A failing system

A brief look at the other aspects of the criminal justice system reveals the problem of remote accountability and poor performance. There is clear evidence that the Crown Prosecution Service is proving ineffective. Seven per cent of cases each year are abandoned 'in error'. By 2000, the CPS was bringing 65 per cent fewer prosecutions against offenders aged 14 to 18 than had been prosecuted in 1984, the year before the CPS was established, despite a significant increase in juvenile crime in the intervening years. Whereas the CPS was established to prevent the dishonesty with evidence which sometimes occurred when the police were the prosecutors, today the opposite problem is occurring. There is a failure of communication, and a culture of blame-passing, between the police and prosecutors, with the result that too many criminals fall between the cracks and victims are denied justice.

As for sentencing, judges and magistrates have responded in recent years to the clear public demand for stiffer sentences by sending criminals to prison earlier in their criminal career and for longer stretches. This is welcome, for it has significantly reduced potential crime through the incapacitation of criminals. And yet if prison works at this most fundamental purpose, it is failing in its secondary, but vital, role of rehabilitation. Over half of all prisoners are reconvicted within two years of their release, including 75 per cent of young offenders under 21 and nearly 90 per cent of those under 18. Prisons are managed by the new National Offender Management Service, comprising the former Prison and Probation Services, under a chief executive accountable to the Home Secretary: another top-heavy, top-down structure which estranges local communities from the public servants supposed to be protecting them against crime.

Send for the Sheriff

Police Authorities should be scrapped. Instead a simple, effective and transparent system of local accountability should be introduced: directly elected individual Sheriffs. Initially, there would be one for each of the 43 police forces in England and Wales; in time, however, it would make sense to bring these forces in line with local government boundaries, thus giving voters a clearer idea of where responsibility lay. Chief Constables would retain operational independence but they would answer to the Sheriff for their performance – and the Commissioner would answer to the public.

Where there was a directly elected Mayor whose jurisdiction was congruent with a police force area (currently only London), the Mayor would exercise the functions of the Sheriff.

Sheriffs would appoint and dismiss Chief Constables. They would set their own targets for the force, make their own Policing Plans, and, crucially, control their own budgets. Each Sheriff would be allocated his or her funding as a block allocation, rather than as a series of micro-managed grants for specific purposes, and would be accountable to local voters for how effectively he or she spent the money in the fight against crime.

Restoring public confidence in the criminal justice system is not simply a question of making those responsible for pursuing criminals through the streets (i.e. the police) more democratically accountable. It is also about making those responsible for pursuing suspects through the courts answerable for their effectiveness in securing convictions, and making those responsible for supervising punishment accountable for their success in protecting the public by reducing re-offending.

We should reconstitute the CPS as a set of local Prosecution Offices, answerable to their local Sheriffs for their success in securing convictions. As in the United States, the Sheriff should not be entitled to order a prosecution, but may order one to be dropped. In order to avoid miscarriages of justice the police and the public prosecution authority should remain distinct and separate entities. However, making them accountable to the same authority would ensure there is greater scope for co-ordination between the two institutions at the sharp end in the fight against crime.

The Sheriff should also be responsible for supervising sentenced criminals. There should be a local purchaser-provider split. Each Sheriff should have responsibility for purchasing space in prisons and other 'disposals' (probation and community punishment capacity), with regard to local wishes. Criminals should serve their sentences – whether in prison or not – under the authority (i.e. as the 'guest') of the Sheriff in the area they committed their crime.

Finally, the Sheriff should have the power to set local sentencing guidelines. While granting an elected official the right to intervene in individual cases would plainly be at odds with the separation of powers, there is no reason why local voters should not have some say over which *categories* of crime to prioritise.

This may well lead to disparities: shop-lifting might lead to incarceration in Kent, but not in Surrey. We suspect that one of two things would then happen. Perhaps Kentish crooks (and crooks of Kent) might pour over the county border in such numbers that the voters of Surrey chose to elect a tougher Sheriff. Or perhaps the voters of Kent, who are also taxpayers, would tire of having to find all the prison places required by their Sheriff's hard line. At which point, the Sheriff of Kent, knowing that he was up for re-election, might try something different. He might rule, for example, that instead of facing jail, shoplifters should be made to stand outside Bluewater with placards around their necks reading 'shoplifter'. We don't know what local people would choose. That is the essence of localism.

The Sheriff's discretionary power over prosecutions will lead to similar incongruities. Different parts of the country might end up with different guidelines on how far a homeowner could go in attacking intruders. It should be noted, however, that discrepancies already exist today: some Chief Constables, for example, decline to treat the possession of cannabis as an offence. The difference is that Chief Constables are not answerable to anybody.

These specific proposals, however, matter less than the philosophy that underlies them. People feel, and with reason, that the legal system no longer functions as the majority would like. John Locke's original compact has been broken: having contracted out our right to personal defence and enforcement, we find that the state no longer fulfils its part of the bargain. The legal system gives the appearance of reflecting the prejudices of an unrepresentative clique of experts in Whitehall, on the Bench and, not least, abroad.

The surest way to address that concern is to bring justice and policing under local democratic control.

3. Parliament should be supreme

➢ Scrap the Human Rights Act
➢ Withdraw from the European Convention on Human Rights
➢ Pass a Reserve Powers Act, guaranteeing the supremacy of
  Parliament against foreign treaties and domestic judicial activism
➢ Appoint senior judges through open parliamentary hearings

Criminal justice represents perhaps the supreme power that the government exercises over the citizen. A state may be defined as a territory whose inhabitants are bound by a common set of laws. Who, though, is to make those laws?

The attempts to answer this question are the chapters that make up the history of modern democracy. Over the past three centuries, European societies have, by and large, adopted the idea that laws ought to be fashioned by representatives of the people; that law-makers, in other words, should be accountable, not *upwards* to ecclesiastical or monarchical powers, but *downwards* to the people expected to live under their rules.

This observation may seem a commonplace. But, in recent years, there has been a trend away from the supremacy of elected legislatures. Laws are increasingly made and enforced by organs of the state that are not accountable to the rest of the populace: the judiciary, autonomous government agencies and, as we saw in the last section, the police.

Elected governments find themselves constrained by a growing corpus of international law. At home, the decisions of elected ministers are habitually overturned by judicial review. Laws, both international and domestic, are stretched by activist courts, which interpret them in a way that their framers could not possibly have envisaged.

Both judges and Chief Constables sometimes talk with startling frankness of their 'duty' to rise above popular prejudice. Yes, say senior judges (when speaking extra-judicially), voters may well want murderers to be banged up for life; but it is up to us to ensure that vote-grabbing Home Secretaries don't pander to tabloid campaigns. Yes, say ambitious Chief Constables, the punters might want us to concentrate on protecting property and cracking down on street crime, but we need to make sure that we are also defending the rights of minorities.

These motives are unexceptionable. The trouble is that the officials concerned are not subjected to any democratic oversight. High Court judges are effectively unsackable: they can be removed only by a joint address by both Houses of Parliament. We are, in short, reverting to the pre-modern concept that law-makers should be accountable to the Crown, to their own consciences, or to God – not to the people affected by their decisions.

Our aim should be to drag justice and home affairs back into the orbital pull of public opinion. There will always be a separation of powers; there will always be a measure of discretion for local officials. But with only a slight recalibration, the balance can be tilted from the executive and judicial branches of government back to the elected legislature. We can, in short, help to restore the principle of representative government that was Britain's greatest contribution to the happiness of mankind.

Constraining judicial activism

Judicial activism – that is, the tendency of judges to rule on the basis of what they think the law ought to say, rather than what it says – is not new. On the contrary, it can hardly fail to exist, in some measure, in any legal system.

In 1717, in a sermon preached before his king, Bishop Hoadly of Winchester observed: 'Whoever hath an absolute authority to interpret any written or spoken laws, it is he who is truly the lawgiver, and not the person who first wrote or spake them.' This is true by definition.

Of course, the frontier between flexibility in interpretation and judicial activism is disputed. Most laws allow a degree of discretion to the courts, correctly recognising that there may otherwise be unintended consequences. Where there are ambiguities or grey areas, judges quite properly apply their common sense.

The problem arises when, in pursuit of what they see as a just settlement, judges deliberately set aside what the statute says. They do so, no doubt, from the highest of motives, seeking to uphold the liberal and humane values of Western society. And there is no question that contemporary politics has witnessed a huge growth in the volume of laws generally, and bad laws particularly. But to disregard the will of Parliament creates a greater wrong than bad law.

What constitutes a breach of the border? At what point does a judge's sense of duty violate the proper relationship between legislature and judiciary? When, in short, do judges become, in Bishop Hoadly's phrase, lawgivers?

Let us glance at a handful of recent cases where a ministerial decision has been struck down by the courts. They serve to indicate how far that frontier has shifted, how much legislative territory has been annexed by the judiciary.

'So draconian that they must be held ultra vires'

In 1996, Michael Howard, as Home Secretary, decided to tackle the problem of illicit entrants to the UK who, often after residing in the country for several years, suddenly claimed to be victims of political persecution when found by the authorities and threatened with deportation. The Social Security (Persons from Abroad) Miscellaneous Amendments Regulations (1996) required asylum seekers to submit their claims as soon as reasonably practicable after arrival in the UK. If they did not do so, but submitted applications only when contesting their repatriation, they would forfeit their entitlement to income support and housing benefit.

The law was immediately challenged by the Joint Council for the Welfare of Immigrants on grounds that it constituted a breach of fundamental human rights (*R* v. *Secretary of State for Social Security, ex parte Joint Council for the Welfare of Immigrants*; *R* v. *Secretary of State for Social Security ex parte B* [1996]). Mr Howard had grounds to be confident: the claimants concerned, after all, were not refugees, and therefore not covered by any of the conventions habitually cited by the courts to overrule him. And, indeed, Simon Brown LJ, in making his ruling acknowledged the problem, although he did not allow it to detain him:

True, no obligation arises under art 24 of the 1951 convention until asylum seekers are recognised as refugees. But that is not to say that up to that point their fundamental needs can be properly ignored. I do not accept that they can.

On what grounds, then, could he strike down a measure that so obviously made him uncomfortable? Why, the very fact that the rules were too harsh:

> *For the purposes of this appeal, however, it suffices to say that I, for my part, regard the 1996 regulations now in force as so uncompromisingly draconian in effect that they must indeed be held* ultra vires.

This seems a remarkable ground on which to overturn Parliament. The judge may have been right that the rules went too far: he is certainly as entitled as anyone else to an opinion. But, feeling as he did, the correct procedure would have been to leave the Bench, stand for election as an MP, persuade a majority of his countrymen to support him and amend the rules.

'Until this court decided otherwise'

Then again, why go to all that trouble when you can simply change the law from the Bench? Consider, as an example, Mohammed Fayed's demand for an explanation when his application for British citizenship was turned down (*R* v. *Secretary of State for the Home Department, ex parte Fayed and another* [1996]).

The case did not involve Mr Fayed's bid for naturalisation, which had previously been refused, along with his brother's. Again, the Home Secretary had every reason to believe that the law was on his side. British nationality is not an automatic entitlement, but a privilege to be bestowed in exceptionally meritorious cases. There is no automatic assumption that it will be granted, so it would be strange indeed to oblige the Home Secretary to explain his reasons when he chose to withhold it.

This is not simply an inference: it is spelt out in the most unequivocal terms by the pertinent statute, the 1981 British Nationality Act, which states: 'The Home Secretary's decision shall not be subject to review in or challenge by any court whatever.'

This sounds pretty final and, indeed, Lord Woolf, in delivering his judgment, accepted that 'the Home Secretary was not obliged to give reasons for refusing an application for British citizenship.' He then went on, however, to argue that the Home Secretary ought to behave fairly and that, in his opinion, this meant giving the applicant sufficient information to make representations. He rounded off his judgment with a statement that ought to alarm anyone who believes in the separation of powers:

> *This decision does not involve any criticism of the Secretary of State or his department. Until this court decided otherwise, it was perfectly reasonable to take a different view. [emphasis added]*

Lord Woolf, significantly, has argued extra-judicially that judges have not only the *right* but the *obligation* to strike down 'bad' laws. Who, though, is to decide what constitutes a bad law? We all have our assumptions and prejudices, judges as much as politicians. The difference is that, if the rest of us disagree with what the politicians have decided, we can remove them.

More flagrant examples

Again and again, we see courts overturning the will of Parliament, set out in the plainest possible language, on the basis of a more or less arbitrary interpretation of what constitutes 'fairness'. The phenomenon is at work in every corner of the judiciary. In 2005, Martin Mears, the first person to be directly elected as President of the Law Society, published a devastating critique of the structural bias against husbands and fathers in the Family Courts (*Institutional Injustice: The Family Courts at work,* Civitas, 2005).

The most high-profile cases, however, usually turn on human rights, the status of minorities and immigration. It is here that jurists seem to feel the strongest obligation to take a stand against what they see as the unconscionable populism of elected politicians.

- In 1997, an illegal immigrant overturned his deportation order on grounds that he would not receive the same medical treatment in his home country as was available in the UK. The court cited Article Three of the European Convention on Human Rights, which reads 'No one shall be subjected to torture or to inhuman or degrading treatment or punishment.' It seems fair to say, to put it as neutrally as possible, that such an interpretation would not have been in the minds of those who drafted the Convention.

- In 2002, another illegal entrant overturned the suspension of her social security payments on grounds that she had not been formally notified that her asylum application had been rejected (she was able to maintain this situation by repeatedly failing to attend the interview).

- In 2004, the Law Lords ruled that the government had no right to intern terror suspects in a 'three-walled prison' in Belmarsh (so called because the detainees were foreign nationals, and were free to return to their countries of origin). With spectacularly bad timing, days before the detonation of a series of bombs on the London Underground on 7 July, Lord Hoffman declared that 'the threat to the life of our nation' came, not from terrorism, 'but from laws such as these'.

- In 2006, HM Inspector of Probation published a report of his review of the case of Anthony Rice, a life sentence prisoner who had murdered a woman called Naomi Bryant following his release from prison on licence. The report found that one of the reasons why the Parole Board freed Rice was that it judged that that human rights legislation required his release.

- Four successive Home Secretaries have struggled to repatriate the Afghan hijackers who arrived in Britain by diverting a flight to Stansted. Each removal order was quashed by the courts, despite the crime the hijackers committed in coming, and despite the fact that Britain had expended a good deal of blood and treasure ridding Afghanistan of the Taliban regime from which they claimed to be fleeing. They are all still in Britain, with full welfare entitlements.

Indeed, to find a converse example from recent years – an example, that is, of the courts stepping in to *order* a deportation – we have to look at the 1998 Law Lords judgment on Augusto Pinochet. General Pinochet had been detained in Britain on a Spanish warrant in connection with charges relating to human rights abuses in Chile.

Whatever the rights and wrongs of the warrant, it seemed clear that Gen Pinochet, as a head of state at the time of the alleged offences, was covered by the doctrine of sovereign immunity. That doctrine is not only affirmed by international convention; it is also written into British statute, as Lord Bingham noted when ordering Gen Pinochet's release.

Lord Bingham's judgment was, however, overruled by the Law Lords, by a vote of three to two, because (according to Lords Steyn and Hoffman) sovereign immunity did not bestow protection from charges relating to human rights abuses, since these did not relate to the proper functions of a head of state. Again, it is hard to avoid the suspicion that the judges were acting according to what they felt the law ought to have said rather than what it said. Lord Hoffman, in particular, was later in trouble for failing to declare his links to Amnesty International, which had long campaigned to bring Gen Pinochet to trial.

Quit the European Convention on Human Rights

The Human Rights Act incorporated the European Convention on Human Rights into British law, thus making it justiciable before UK courts. Before the Act, petitions had to go directly to the European Court of Human Rights in Strasbourg.

Repealing the Human Rights Act and un-incorporating the ECHR from UK law, without a simultaneous abrogation of the Convention itself, would simply mean that Parliament was overruled by foreign rather than domestic judges. True, unsupported repeal might slightly reduce the scale of judicial activism. In the 21 years between 1975 and 1996, the European Convention had been considered in 316 cases and affected the outcome, reasoning or procedure in 16 of them. In the 18 months between October 2000 (when the Act came into force) and April 2002, the ECHR was substantively considered in 431 cases in the higher courts, and affected the outcome, reasoning and procedure in 318. But repealing the Human Rights Act would not necessarily mean a return to the *status quo ante*. For our own courts have now got a taste for citing the Convention.

In the official inquiry into the early release of Anthony Rice, this phenomenon was called a 'human rights culture'. Many public institutions, not just the Parole Board, are affected. There is no reason to expect their attitudes to change as long as they can reasonably contend that the UK remains bound by precisely the same charter as the one currently incorporated by the Human Rights Act.

No, half-hearted repeal would be the worst kind of declamatory politics: a measure designed to signal the government's toughness rather than to alter anything.

A genteel coup d'état

Squint impressionistically at the problem of judicial activism, and two features become immediately apparent. First, the skewing of the plain wording of the law always seems to happen in the same political direction. Second, creative interpretation has been enormously exacerbated by the growth of a corpus of international human rights law.

Robert Bork, whose nomination to the US Supreme Court was blocked by the Senate in 1987, has studied the ballooning of international jurisprudence since the early 1990s, and concluded that it amounts to a sustained attempt to impose on states from above laws and values that would never have passed through their national parliaments.

'What judges have wrought is a *coup d'état,*' he writes in *Coercing Virtue: The Worldwide Rule of Judges*, 'slow-moving and genteel, but a *coup d'état* nonetheless.'

Slow-moving, genteel, and from the Left. We have already discussed the determination of judges always and everywhere to block deportation orders. But when did you last read of a court stepping in to demand the removal of an illegal entrant who had improperly been granted leave to remain?

We are familiar with the outrage provoked whenever a Home Secretary rules that a high-profile murderer ought not to be eligible for parole. Politicians, chorus a line-up of retired judges, ought not to interfere in the judicial process. Yet we did not hear a squeak when, in a massive and blatant interference in the judicial process, the Home Secretary ordered that dozens of convicted terrorists be released early from their sentences under the terms of the 1998 Belfast Agreement.

Likewise, the attempt by Parliament to set minimum tariffs for certain offences is inevitably decried by the courts as a monstrous assault on judicial independence and a threat to the separation of powers. Yet the setting by Parliament of *maximum* tariffs seems to raise no constitutional questions whatever.

As we have already seen, standing bureaucracies tend to be well to the Left of the electorate, and judges are no exception. When people read of prisoners being paid £50,000 compensation for having to slop out their cells, or drug addicts claiming compensation for not being given substitute narcotics in prison, or al-Qa'eda suspects successfully blocking their extradition to countries where they are wanted on terrorist offences, they understandably conclude that the judiciary seems to care for the human rights of scoundrels rather than those of honest men.

Right-wing dictators only, please

The phenomenon can be seen at international level, too. Writs are now routinely served, not only against dictators such as Pinochet, but against Ariel Sharon, Donald Rumsfeld and other controversial conservatives. Oddly, no one tried to indict Yasser Arafat, Fidel Castro or Robert Mugabe.

The internationalisation of criminal justice has been one of the main drivers of judicial activism within states. When judges can find no domestic statute to justify the rulings they would like to make, they reach instead for the European Convention or one of many UN accords.

The notion of international law is not new. It has existed in something like its present form since the end of the Second World War. Prior to that, the phrase 'international law' referred simply to the mediation of relations among states, not to their domestic behaviour. William Blackstone defined offences against international law as the violation of safe conduct passes, the mistreatment of ambassadors and piracy.

As we shall see, the foundation of the United Nations and the Nuremberg trials substantially widened the definition of international jurisdiction. But the real revolution has come since, and largely as a consequence of, the end of the Cold War. This revolution has fundamentally altered the relationship between national legislatures and their judiciaries. It is to this global rise of the judges that we now turn.

The internationalisation of law

In 2001, Henry Kissinger made a startling observation:

In less than a decade, an unprecedented concept has emerged to submit international politics to judicial procedures. It has spread with extraordinary speed and has not been subject to systematic debate, partly because of the intimidating passion of its advocates... The danger is that it is being pushed to extremes which risk substituting the tyranny of judges for that of governments; historically, the dictatorship of the virtuous has often led to inquisitions and even witch-hunts.

Kissinger is right. There has been a huge growth in international criminal law since the end of the Cold War. The process started in 1990, when, on 11 September, President George H. W. Bush proclaimed 'a new world order'. What he meant was that United Nations Security Council Resolutions could be enforced by means of military force, since the East–West division in Europe and the hostility between the USA and the USSR had been overcome and the deadlock in the Security Council lifted. The United Nations would henceforth be able to call on its members to fight wars on its behalf, thereby giving international law a coercive quality which it had never had before.

The phrase 'new world order' did not originate with the Americans, however. It had been reintroduced into political discourse by the outgoing Soviet president, Mikhail Gorbachev, who rekindled the old Trotskyite dream of world government by calling for global governance and a unification of the world economy. Soon, the Left-wing and globalist origins of the 'new world order' project became clear: institutions proliferated at international level pursuing an overtly anti-conservative agenda and transferring ever more power away from ordinary people into obscure and unaccountable international institutions.

The change was put well by a Prosecutor at the Yugoslav War Crimes tribunal, Louise Arbour, who said in 1999, 'We have passed from an era of co-operation between states into an era in which states can be constrained.' The sentiment may be noble but it immediately prompts the question: 'Who is to check the powers of the person doing the constraining?'

Prior to the proclamation of the 'new world order', international law consisted essentially of treaties between states. States were free agents which concluded contracts one with another. Occasionally, they created large institutions such as the United Nations to oversee the terms of their agreements, and occasionally the terms of the treaties were based on appeals to universal values such as the Conventions on Genocide or Torture. But none of these treaties gave rise to systems of coercive law comparable to the national law of a state, enforced by the police and the courts. Any penalties imposed for treaty violations were accepted voluntarily by the states that had signed them.

Moreover, to the extent that international treaties created obligations, those obligations concerned only states, not individuals. The Genocide and Torture Conventions, for instance, require *national* bodies to pursue persons suspected of these crimes.

European rights and wrongs

The big exception to this general rule was the European Union. The EU differs from other treaty organisations in that its law penetrates into the very fabric of national life, imposing obligations on individuals. This is why the EU's power is so awesome. Once the 'new world order' was proclaimed, however, the EU model was copied by other international bodies, and soon a host of international organisations had cropped up which claimed the right to regulate the most intimate details of people's lives from on high.

The main vehicle for this internationalisation of law has been the doctrine of 'universal human rights'. In the name of statements of desirable general principles, international organisations have been created which claim the right to interpret and even to enforce those principles as they see fit. People often react favourably when they hear that a new body has been created to protect human rights. What they perhaps do not realise is that ordinary people do not get any new rights as a result. Rather, it is the people working in the new institution who get the right to say what ordinary people's rights are.

The EU has been trying to gain control over 'human rights' for years. The European heads of state and government signed the Charter of Fundamental Rights and Freedoms at Nice in 2000. Strictly speaking, the charter has no legal force. It *would* have become legally binding if the European

Constitution had been adopted, since the Charter formed an integral part of it, but the Constitution was rejected in referendums in France and the Netherlands in 2005. But the EU was not going to allow a little thing like a 'No' vote to deter it. Its various institutions simply declared the Charter to be in force, and the European Court of Justice treated it as justiciable. In March 2007, the EU created an Agency for Fundamental Rights, based in Vienna, whose remit was to enforce the Charter.

This is an example of how the EU puts in place institutions even when it has been explicitly denied the legal right to do so by voters. There are few clearer illustrations of how, like the sorcerer's apprentice, the peoples of Europe have allowed an institution to be created, the EU, which has taken on a life of its own and which they can no longer control.

The new Agency will have only an advisory role for the time being, but its remit is huge: the Charter of Fundamental Rights, on which the Agency's so-called 'mandate' is based, contains rules on everything – on the right to life, on liberty, on the right to a fair trial and on the right to a family. There are rules on data protection, consumer protection, environmental protection, freedom of thought, freedom of religion. There is 'the freedom of the arts' and 'the right to education'. Asylum policy, multiculturalism, social security, health care, the right to vote – you name it, the EU has a policy on it. There is even a 'right to good administration' – which is pretty rich, coming from Brussels.

In addition to this, in February 2007, the European Commission put forward a proposal which would allow Brussels to send people to prison for polluting the environment. No doubt pollution is a bad thing, but are we really prepared to give the power of imprisonment to the same organisation which for fifty years has run the corrupt, wasteful and partly criminal Common Agricultural Policy?

Enforcing rights at gunpoint

The 1990s also saw the birth of the doctrine of military interventionism. Like the doctrine of universal human rights on which it is based, humanitarian interventionism is a doctrine with superficial appeal but which unfortunately is wide open to abuse. Interdependence was shown to be a grim reality when intervention over Kosovo in 1999 caused huge numbers of Albanian asylum seekers to arrive in this country. On the backs of the doctrine of interventionism, two international criminal tribunals were created, one for Yugoslavia and the other for Rwanda. Now a third court, the International Criminal Court, has been created. It has the power to prosecute national leaders, including national leaders in this country, and this is a power which will inevitably be politically abused. It is precisely for this reason that the Americans have sensibly not signed the ICC Charter.

Many people think it is right and proper that unscrupulous heads of state should end up in the dock if they have committed crimes. But who is to prosecute them? If the argument is that leaders should be democratically accountable for their acts, then obviously it is their national courts which should bring any such prosecutions. There is nothing democratic about taking away the rights of states to prosecute their own leaders and investing them instead in unaccountable international tribunals. International tribunals are not elected and they are not accountable to the people over whom they have jurisdiction. The Yugoslav and Rwanda tribunals have now become a law unto themselves, prosecuting some men for no better reason than that it was thought politically expedient to have indictees from all sides in a war. The abuses of due process in these new tribunals are so grave that one of the ICTY's judges, a distinguished Australian, has said that its rules will leave 'a spreading stain on the Tribunal's reputation'. Is this really the kind of comment we expect from a Tribunal supposed to uphold the highest standards?

The problem in all such cases is the problem expressed by the oldest question in political philosophy, *Quis custodiet ipsos custodes?* Since the beginning of civilisation, people have dreamed of a rationally ordered republic governed by wise philosopher kings. However, who is to prevent the philosopher kings from abusing their powers, and who is to say that their decisions will necessarily be approved by the people? If the principle of democratic accountability is to mean anything, then the link must be re-established between the people who make laws, on the one hand, and the people who are governed by them and who pay for their implementation, on the other. In other words, the internationalisation of law should cease. Law-making and law-enforcement powers should be returned to national courts and national authorities.

The reader may feel that we have spent a long time on this subject. After all, international law-codes and judicial activism are not high on most voters' lists of concerns. But when the European Convention is used to secure early prisoner releases, to prevent the deportation of terror suspects, or to order changes in employment law, voters' reaction is immediate and angry. If you do not believe us, go canvassing.

The issues that most irk people on the doorstep cannot be addressed without tackling the burgeoning jurisprudence of international courts. Pull out the Human Rights Act and, like a deep-rooted weed, it will draw up behind it a series of international codes and conventions. Only when Parliament is sovereign over supra-national jurists, as well as domestic courts, will it be in a position to deliver a settlement that voters regard as just.

4. State schools should be independent

➤ Central government should cease to dictate administration and teaching policies to local schools
➤ The national curriculum should be scrapped
➤ Parents of school-aged children should be given a new legal right allowing them to take their custom to schools not controlled by the state, carrying with them the money that would have been spent on their children by the Local Education Authority
➤ This financial credit should be determined by the per capita average spent on each child by their local authority, according to the type of school
➤ Priority should be given to children with Special Educational Needs when implementing the reform.

Britain's education system is failing. A gap has opened between the virtual world of ever-improving GCSE results and the real world of remedial teaching offered by universities and employers to bring school-leavers up to the standard of previous generations. Consider the following statistics:

- 75,000 children finish formal education each year having failed to achieve five GCSEs at any grade, and one in ten 16-year-olds leaves school without a single qualification
- Fewer than half of those sitting GCSEs in English and Maths gained grades higher than D
- A quarter of children leave primary school without the necessary reading and writing skills to tackle the secondary school curriculum, and three out of every ten children do not reach the levels they need in English, Maths and Science to sit their GCSEs
- British schoolchildren have fallen steadily down the league tables of academic ability and are now close to the bottom of the class among the world's democracies

On top of poor academic standards, poor standards of pupil behaviour have become endemic in many schools. Parents are beginning to realise what teachers have complained of for years: that adults are losing control of the classroom.

This alarming picture of failure in our education system has been hidden by changes in the exam and school testing systems used. The tools for assessing a child's performance rarely involve measuring his or her performance against other children nationally, and never against similarly aged children in previous years or other countries. While the government trumpets improvements in exam grades, employers and university admissions tutors report a sharp decline in standards.

Exam grades are suffering inflation for the same reason that currencies do: the government is too loose in its control of the supply. Too many pupils do too many exams designed to get them into too many universities where there are too many degrees on offer to too many students.

The trouble is that it suits most people to go along with the notion that humankind – at least in England and Wales – is getting steadily cleverer. Schools like to trumpet their grades. Teachers' organisations like to point to their success. Ministers like to pat themselves on the back for their stewardship of the system. Parents like to congratulate their children. Pupils are understandably proud of their achievements. It would be a brave politician who offended all these groups by pointing at international comparitors, or at old O-level questions that are being recycled into A-level papers.

Why schools fail

Our schools are failing because of too much government. Government decides how many schools there are in your area. Government draws up the rules that decide where your children go to school, what they learn there, how they are taught. Government determines who can teach and how teachers are trained. Government decides how many hours your children spend on different subjects, what they eat, how they behave.

Government provides a near monopoly of education. And as with any monopoly, those who use the service – parents and children – have little choice. That is why schools fail; and that is why, when they fail, so little is done to put things right.

The state monopoly means uniformity – and mediocrity – across the education system. The reins of big government have tightened with a national curriculum, the *de facto* nationalisation of exam boards, and funding initiatives that dictate not simply what a school must do, but how it must do it. Most recently, a 'sustainable schools' agenda now dictates the very shape of the school buildings and classrooms themselves.

For all but the seven per cent who are able to afford a private education, what ministers decide is what they have to accept. The vast majority of people in Britain are forced to take what the government provides for their child and are expected to be grateful.

Education is thus truly a postcode lottery. That phrase is often used loosely to indicate regional disparities, but in this case it is exactly apt. We are allocated our postcodes, and have no say over whether we win a lottery. The quality of a child's education can depend on his proximity to a particular school; and local parents have no mechanism to affect what happens within that school.

A few families, unable to afford to go private, and unhappy with their local school, might still be able to afford to move home. But this minority is not large, and indicative of a greater number who are unhappy but do not complain. Each year around one in ten parents appeals against a local authority decision to send a child to a particular school, though only a quarter of those appeals are upheld. The problem is more acute in inner cities, where nearly 20 per cent of admission decisions are appealed against, but less than 20 per cent of appeals are successful.

Over-subscription requires popular schools to introduce admissions criteria to enable them to choose between applicants. There are several non-academic methods which schools may use to select their pupils, including informal methods such as an interview or assessing the parents' religious observance for faith-based schools.

The most common form of selection for the majority of popular schools is a simple and objective one: the 'proximity rule', or catchment area. Catchment areas obviously mean that schools tend to reflect the community mix that lives around them. This is especially true of schools in rural areas. However, in towns and cities, catchment areas often make for less mixed schools. At their worst, catchment areas can mean that the localities of good schools become enclaves of the rich, while areas around bad schools become ghettos of the poor. Lauriston Primary School in Hackney, for example, has a catchment area that extends no more than 110 yards from the school gates. As a result, houses close to the school sell for over £100,000 more than others down the road.

Catchment areas are simply a form of rationing limited resources – places in good schools. Too many parents want places in schools they perceive to be good, and not enough choose schools in places they perceive to be bad. Arbitrary boundaries, therefore, are used to prevent parents taking their children out of one school and putting them into another.

Rather than have a system that simply rations the limited number of places in good schools, why not have one that increases the number of good schools and the number of places in such schools?

Too many of the ideas that politicians have about education seek only to deal with the consequences of a system that lacks choice. Promising to impose synthetic phonics, or a more rigorous curriculum, or healthier eating, or more discipline, is to offer to make schools produce the outcomes that parents want. Why not instead tackle the cause of the problem, the inability of the schools themselves to provide what parents want? Rather than politicians promising to give parents what they want, why not give parents the ability to ensure that schools provide their children with a real education?

In short, having diagnosed the problem as bad management by the state, we need to prescribe an appropriate and proportionate remedy.

Where the Right went wrong

Aha, you cry, but there *is* an appropriate remedy. It has been kicking around for more than half a century and, although it has been applied in practice in very few instances, these instances have on the whole been hugely successful.

The remedy is to set all schools free from state control, to allow them to compete for custom, and to provide prospective parents with the wherewithal to use them in the form of education credits.

For a long time, conservatives called this policy 'vouchers'. Then, finding that voters found the v-word intimidating and wonkish, they shifted their language. Today, they prefer to talk about 'choice'.

V-word or c-word, the policy has obvious attractions. In every other sphere of life, the removal of government tends to lead to enterprise, diversity and growth. We no longer expect politicians to be especially good at building cars or installing telephones, so why should they be any better at running schools?

In any case, no minister, however well-disposed, can anticipate the needs and interests of every child in the land. That child's parents will, in general, be better placed to judge his or her needs. And schools, freed from the expense and the nuisance of state targets and LEA meddling, will be able to focus their attention on their primary task.

True, some bad schools could fold for lack of custom, and the impact of such closures may be painful for children who are displaced and forced to settle in somewhere new. But how much worse is it to leave a failing school open, blighting the prospects of generation after generation?

All these arguments have merit. But the policy of 'school choice' has two serious drawbacks, one strategic and one tactical.

The strategic drawback is that any national voucher scheme is open to being manipulated, distorted or terminated by an ill-disposed government. Schools can be brought relatively painlessly back under LEA control, as we saw after the 1997 election when Labour swiftly did away with Grant Maintained Schools.

Even if a future government shied away from outright abolition, there would be many ways in which it could traduce a voucher scheme, by making schools follow a certain curriculum or particular admissions policies in order to qualify. New Labour has already set such a precedent in the field of higher education, obliging universities to follow particular admissions criteria in order to be eligible for the income from tuition fees. Even more strikingly, it has done the same with nursery vouchers, on one occasion threatening to withdraw its recognition from a nursery because it was spending too much time teaching infants to read.

The tactical objection is, quite simply, that voters do not seem especially keen on freedom when applied to the field of education. 'I don't want choice,' is a frequently heard complaint; 'what I want is a good school at the end of my road.' Vainly does the Centre-Right politician protest that choice is there precisely as a mechanism to lift standards. Vainly does he try to convince the voter that, if all restaurants were owned by the state, their food would be indifferent, and that it is precisely because we are able to choose which restaurant to patronise that we are likely to have a decent one 'at the end of our road'. By the time a candidate finds himself making these arguments, he has already lost.

Applying localist principles

How, then, can we solve the problems inherent in a state monopoly while taking account of these two objections? Is there a way to increase school freedom and to raise standards without a full-scale voucher scheme? And can such a policy be made not just electorally saleable, but positively popular?

For an answer, it is instructive to consider what was arguably the single most popular policy pursued by the last Conservative Government, namely the sale of council houses.

For much of the twentieth century, the provision of housing was seen, as the provision of education is today, as chiefly an activity for the state. Of course there was private housing, just as there are private schools, but most people expected to look, in the first instance, to their local authority.

Margaret Thatcher's government shifted most of the housing stock from the state to the independent sector, not by a mass privatisation scheme, but by entitling council tenants to buy their way out of government control. The policy of council house sales was more successful than the sell-offs of state companies and utilities on at least two grounds. First, it was more popular. The denationalisation of vast assets was accomplished with almost none of the controversy that later attended the sale of, for example, water or rail companies. Second, and partly as a consequence, it was effectively irreversible. It is conceivable that a future government could renationalise other utilities, as has already happened to Railtrack. But it is impossible to imagine the mass expropriation of now privately-owned homes.

Unusually, a government of the Right did something that is more commonly achieved by the Left: it created a corpus of voters with a vested interest in maintaining its legacy. What Labour Governments have done with huge success by expanding the state payroll, swelling welfare dependency and creating quangos to maintain their statutes, the Tories have done just once, albeit with genius, in the field of housing.

Applied to the field of education, the traditional voucher scheme may be likened to the mass privatisations of the later Thatcher years. The equivalent of the sale of council houses would be to give every parent with school-age children the right to demand, from his local authority, the sum that it would have spent on his child, and to take that sum where he pleases.

This sum would plainly vary according to the age and circumstances of the child. To reach a rough equivalence, primary and secondary schools and sixth-form colleges should be differentiated, as should Special Schools. Each child would be entitled to the average spent per pupil in the appropriate sector – calculated by dividing the entire budget by the number of children in the system, and without making any deductions (the salaries of LEA officials, for example, should be counted as part of the budget).

A legal entitlement for parents

Currently, parents may apply to state schools in their area in a process which is mediated by the LEA, which also funds local schools. Some parents are happy with this arrangement. Many, however, are plainly not, as may be seen both from opinion surveys and from the number of appeals against the allocation of school places. Parents who want to opt out should be given direct control over their child's share of the funds.

Opponents of parental choice might argue that parents are not always best qualified to exercise choice. While we do not accept this argument, it is certainly the case that if responsibility is taken away from people, they tend to behave less responsibly. Parents have, by and large, been denied responsibility for their child's education, with too many decisions made for them in our 'like-it-or-lump-it' education system.

With a legal entitlement, parents who were dissatisfied with the level of provision that their child was getting could exercise it. Parents who were content with what their child was getting – or in some cases even apathetic about their child's education – would be no worse off. Those parents who did want to take more responsibility for their child's education could do so.

The precise mechanism by which that control is exercised, and the definition of 'their child's share', need not be laid down by Whitehall. Once a legal right has been enshrined, it could be left to parents, using the courts and judicial fiat, to do the rest – that is, to determine how a local authority should meet its legal obligation.

If a local authority does not believe that funds received by parents are being used for the purposes of education, as laid down in primary legislation, it should be for a court to decide this matter – just as a court decides whether a car sold to a customer is fit for purpose in the event of a dispute. Before the regulatory age, this is how such matters were decided, across a whole range of applications in the UK. It was an approach compatible with our common law system and it was enormously successful.

Parents have a moral right to decide how their children should be educated. We should enshrine this right in law. Anything more risks wrapping up an ostensibly liberated system in unnecessary regulation.

Special needs education

We recommend starting the scheme to help children with Special Educational Needs, who have been most failed by the *status quo*. It is here that parents are suffering most from the existing system, and where there is the strongest demand for the right to pick the schools which are best suited to a child's circumstances. Once the principle is seen to be working, the same right could be swiftly extended to all parents. This would largely anticipate the reflexive complaint about any loosening up of the education monopoly, namely that such freedom is simply a way to subsidise Eton and Harrow fees.

The extent to which parents of children with special needs have no choice has been highlighted by the controversy over the closure of Special Schools. While many parents of children with special needs prefer their child to attend a Special School, ideologically motivated educationalists have favoured 'inclusion' – a policy of aggressively integrating those with special needs into mainstream schools at almost any cost to the wellbeing of the child.

A relatively simple change could ensure that children with special needs had a form of legal entitlement. The 'statementing' process, through which the needs of the child are assessed by local education officials, could be modified. Instead of merely stating what level of additional help and support a child with special needs was entitled to, as at present, statementing could be changed to include a level of financial entitlement to which the child's parent could lay claim.

This would not simply resolve the present debate as to the merits or otherwise of including special needs children in mainstream schools, but it would also open the way towards a general system of entitlement.

Would such a scheme not massively expand the pressure to increase SEN funding? At present some £4.5 billion a year is spent on providing Special Educational Needs, and of that total, some 69 per cent of resources go to children with statements. Our proposal would not *per se* mean any expansion in this budget. It would, however, ensure that the budget was spent on actually delivering help to children who needed it.

What if more parents started to demand the rights enjoyed by parents of children with statements? It is true that some parents might start to demand the same rights to control their child's pot of money as those with statements – and all the better if they did. It would demonstrate that the scheme worked and that choice helped the more vulnerable the most.

Why localism is better than a national voucher scheme
A voucher scheme is a national mechanism; a local opt-out is a legal right. In other words, localism avoids the complicated and technical questions of how to administer a school choice programme. It specifies the outcome rather than the process.

To return to the council house sales analogy, the Thatcher Government did not remove housing stock from local authorities and then seek to allocate one home per applicant. Rather, it gave people the right to buy, and then trusted to the wisdom of the market to do the rest.

The closest overseas equivalent to what we propose can be found in Denmark. In the nineteenth century, an education minister who was also a Lutheran clergyman introduced the principle of match funding for independently run schools. This principle has been respected in subsequent legislation, most recently the 1991 reforms, which specify that pupils in private schools should get the per capita average being spent within the state system. Around 13 per cent of Danish children are in such schools, and there is a broad consensus that their existence pushes up standards in the state schools. Private schools are allowed to levy top-up fees, although these are usually less than £1,000 a year.

Precisely because the Danish system is not a nationally controlled voucher, it is largely immune to government manipulation. The Danish state cannot demand that independent schools follow a particular approach to, say, religious instruction or citizenship classes. Its role is limited to ensuring that pupils at these schools meet the required standards in public examinations. In other words, it lays down a minimal regulation of outcomes, but does not busy itself with process.

This, incidentally, is the answer to one of the more commonly asked questions about autonomous schools, namely 'Would parents be allowed to claim their financial entitlement and then send their children to, say, the Osama bin Laden Madrassah?' Provided that children were reaching the required educational standards, it would not be up to the invigilators to concern themselves with the values or ethos of the school, except insofar as these infracted the law. (A school that was stirring up racial or religious hatred would be breaking not just the recent legislation specifically defining these crimes but also the much older law against incitement. If this were to happen, it would be a matter not for the local council but for the police.)

It is no coincidence that the Danish system has proved so durable. Although the Social Democrats have dominated political life in that country, emerging as the largest party at every post-war election until 2001, the party cannot afford to alienate the parents of that 13 per cent who use independent schools at no additional cost to the taxpayer. It is a fight not worth having.

The same is true of Sweden, where the Social Democrats have been in power for 66 of the past 75 years. During one of the intermissions in 1992, Carl Bildt's short-lived Centre-Right Government introduced a municipal school choice policy. Again, the central government confined itself to laying down the overall objective, leaving local councils to decide how to implement the scheme. Initially, the entitlement was for 85 per cent of the cost of a state place. When the Social Democrats returned to power, they increased the value to 100 per cent, but banned top-up fees. Although they had opposed the scheme in opposition, they found it politically impractical to scrap it when in power.

As well as durability, the localisation of the scheme offers the advantage of pluralism. Different approaches can be trialled, and those that are most successful can be copied, so that best practice spreads. And, because bureaucracies tend to become more remote and less efficient in proportion to their size, a local entitlement would almost certainly prove more cost-effective than a nationally administered voucher scheme.

Encouraging new provision

In order to encourage providers to come forward and offer new places, there will need to be some further amendments to current education policy, consequent on the legal entitlement to funding. First, the Surplus Places Rule will need to be abolished, so that good schools can grow. Of course, many schools do not wish to grow – and many schools are unable to, at least on their existing sites. However, it is noteworthy that the number of children attending Britain's grammar schools grew by over a third between 1993 and 2003. This is equivalent to 46 new grammar schools – but on the existing sites, for no new grammar schools were created in that period. This shows what can be done in response to local pressure on the best schools in an area.

At present, planning rules effectively prevent existing schools from expanding and new schools from being established. There would need to be a review of planning rules to make it easier to obtain local planning permission from the local authority than at present.

Liberating state schools would also allow the all-important freedom to fail. Schools which do not attract sufficient parents will not, as at present, be propped up by the government and allowed to persist in mediocrity, to the permanent damage of those children (often from the most marginalised families) who still attend. Failure would see the school transferred to alternative management, or sold and the proceeds applied to other local schools.

Translating state schools into the independent sector will open them up to competition from new entrants. Again, other countries show the way. In the United States, independently-run, non-profit, non-religious charter schools may be established at the behest of local parents, their charters being awarded by local government, the local university or dedicated charter boards. In the Netherlands, the country's constitution allows any non-profit school run by parents, a charity or church to receive funding (including capital costs) on the same basis as state schools: in consequence, nearly 70 per cent of Dutch schools are independent.

Britain should follow these examples. Indeed, it would be following its own history: public education in this country arose as the private initiative of religious and charitable foundations. Many state-funded schools today, even if they are subject to direction from central and local government, are nominally owned and run by independent institutions, including churches, charities and private businesses. They need to be liberated once again – and subjected to the healthy competition of new entrants.

Because of the effect of the government near-monopoly, private initiative in education has been dormant for decades – but it can be awakened. In the 17 years since per capita funding entitlement was introduced in Sweden, the number of independent schools has more than quadrupled. And in Britain there is considerable commercial and philanthropic appetite for setting up new schools.

In line with international experience we can expect a large proportion of new entrants to be charitable concerns, whether religious foundations or otherwise. Evidence from the United States, in particular – where charter schools are forbidden from distributing profits, which shows that it is not the profit motive which has driven progress – suggests that there is a largely untapped reservoir of money, energy and talent in Britain ready to be committed to education for education's sake.

However, there can be no objection to the profit principle in education. Financiers looking for a return on investments are the natural source of the capital needed for the establishment of new schools, which would otherwise have to come from the taxpayer; and shareholders are the most effective guarantee of high standards and good management. In Sweden, chains of profit-making schools, educating tax-funded pupils, are a particular feature of the system.

Axe the national curriculum

As well as facilitating the development of new schools, central government would have to relinquish the right to dictate the syllabus. This means abolishing the national curriculum. Politicians pretend that the national curriculum ensures children are properly taught. In truth, it is a modern invention which ensures that children are taught a good deal of dross.

The national curriculum – designed to stop wacky Left-wing teachers filling children's heads with nonsense – has been captured by the very people it was supposed to frustrate. It is now a principal method by which the Left-leaning educational establishment imposes its orthodoxies on schools. It is so large that there is insufficient time in the school day for alternative lessons or subjects, and teachers complain that their professional discretion is curtailed.

Exams should be the method by which schools' curricula are kept up to the mark and in line with each other. Private prep schools have no national curriculum, but they know that their reputation rests on their pupils' success in the Common Entrance exams. Standards and commonality will be better preserved in a liberal system than a closed one.

Set our schools free

The idea of localism in education reflects the philosophy that infuses the entire direct democracy agenda. We believe that decisions should be exercised as closely as possible to the people they affect, and that power should be devolved to the lowest practicable unit. When it comes to picking a school, that unit is the individual parent. When it comes to deciding what a school should teach, what admissions criteria it should apply, what uniform policy it should adopt and so on, the unit is the school. When it comes to the financing and invigilation of the system, the unit is the county or city. Only when it comes to specifying the overall level of attainment expected by school leavers is there a role for central government.

Parliament, in other words, should confine itself to setting down the basics of what we expect pupils to know when they leave the classroom for the last time. As to how to get there, MPs have no more expertise than anyone else. Schools themselves are best placed to see what works. Some of their initiatives will be more successful than others. Provided that parents are free to pick the schools that they judge the most successful, best practice will spread.

Thus, millions of individual decisions, made by those with the strongest possible interest in the welfare of their own children, will serve to police and improve the system. No minister, be he the best and wisest in Whitehall, can achieve so much. No committee, no hundred committees sitting night and day, can deliver such an outcome. Give parents local control, and they will do the rest.

5. True localism

➤ Abolish regional development agencies, regional government offices and all regional assemblies, and transfer their powers to local councils
➤ Scrap the Department of Communities and Local Government and pass its powers, too, to local authorities
➤ Grant English counties and cities responsibility for all areas of policy which, under the 1998 Scotland Act, are devolved to the Holyrood Parliament
➤ Replace VAT with a Local Sales Tax
➤ Make local councils self-financing

Local government barely has a pulse. At the last set of local elections, of those who had registered to vote, 64 per cent declined to cast their ballots. Of the remaining 36 per cent, few voted in the hope that it would improve

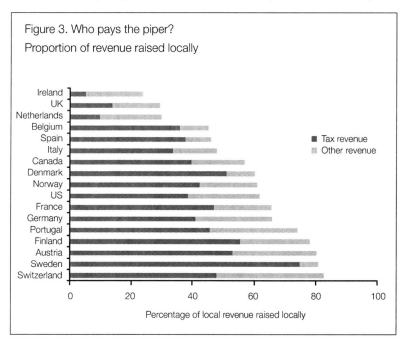

Figure 3. Who pays the piper?
Proportion of revenue raised locally

their neighbourhoods: most were using the election purely to register their dislike of one or another of the national parties.

A revival of genuine civic democracy is the prerequisite for restoring honour and trust to our political system. In the first instance, this is a question of money.

As Figure 3 shows, town halls in Britain are uniquely dependent on subsidies from central government. Of all the countries in Europe, only Ireland, with a population barely more than four per cent of that of the UK, has a more centralised form of local government finance.

Ninety per cent of all revenue collected in Britain goes to the Chancellor in Whitehall. Seventy-five per cent of the money spent locally comes from the Treasury. There is virtually no link between taxation, representation and expenditure at local level. This disconnection has several malign consequences.

1. It rewards inefficiency.
The Treasury's allocation of grants to local government is made on the basis of assessing councils' spending needs against the actual level of local services. Perversely, a local authority that is good at turning revenue into local services does not qualify for as large a grant as an inefficient one. This is one of the reasons that the massive increases in council tax in recent years have not been matched by any corresponding increase in the provision of local services

2. It erodes accountability.
Voters are in no position to reward or punish the behaviour of their local council. It is far from clear who is responsible for what, and who pays. Local elections become an unedifying slanging match as the parties try to blame tax rises on the national government or on each other.

3. It reduces choice.
Political parties are not able to offer radically different manifestos, since they have only limited control over the council's budget. To the extent that they do have the opportunity to promise things, the cost of those things is grossly

distorted by the fact that three-quarters of the budget comes from Whitehall. Thus, a 10 per cent increase in council spending means a 40 per cent rise in council tax.

4. It alienates voters.
Opinion polls show that over 90 per cent of people are dissatisfied with the services provided by their local authority, and that almost 60 per cent believe that their council fails to provide value for money. Voters, in other words, are angry rather than apathetic. Yet turnout at local elections in England and Wales over the past decade has been around 35 per cent. Why? Because people correctly perceive that there is little connection between how they vote and the level of services they receive, or how much they pay for those services. International comparisons support this analysis: in France, where local authorities raise 65 per cent of their own revenue, turnout is normally just over 60 per cent. In Switzerland, where it is 80 per cent, turnout is around 75 per cent.

5. It deters good candidates.
There is less of an incentive for people to enter local politics knowing that they will wield little meaningful power. Someone standing for local government must be willing to be nannied and micro-managed by a distant bureaucracy. Indeed, getting yourself elected can sometimes mean that you have *less* influence than you had before: there have been several cases where the preposterous rules introduced by John Prescott on conflicts of interest have been interpreted to mean that councillors may not speak or vote on issues of relevance to their own wards.

6. It boosts big government.
Whitehall imposes minimum standards of local service provision, without setting ceilings on the maximum level of service provision. This favours local politicians standing on the basis that the town halls should do more, not less. Whitehall's assessment of local authority needs means that those who do not spend 'up to cap' may be penalised with a reduced grant. High-spending politicians have the ready-made excuse that Whitehall is to

blame if local services do not seem adequate. Above all, inept Labour councils are never held to account. The more misery and destitution they cause through their mismanagement, the more Whitehall money they attract, and the more people become dependent on such grants, making them likelier to vote Labour.

Making councils self-financing – albeit allowing for a national top-up for deprived areas – would make them more efficient, more accountable and more attractive to candidates of real quality. But new taxes are never popular. The losers from any reform are unforgiving, while the winners take their gain for granted. This is especially true in the field of local government finance since, for many people, it is the only tax that they have to pay themselves, rather than having it deducted at source through VAT, PAYE or National Insurance. Hence the explosiveness of the issue, as Margaret Thatcher found when she introduced the Poll Tax.

If local government is to raise its own revenue, the method used must be transparent, fair and efficient. Any new tax should visibly replace an existing one rather than simply being an additional impost. And, not least, it should apply evenly to the electorate.

The problem with most mooted forms of local government tax is that each one would leave a goodly proportion of local residents unaffected. Council tax falls disproportionately on those who own houses, but have no income, particularly pensioners; a local income tax would have the opposite flaw, penalising those in work while leaving a large minority wholly exempt; the community charge weighed especially heavily on the working poor. Under any of these systems, a chunk of the electorate would be encouraged to vote for higher spending, knowing that they would be unaffected by the consequential tax rises.

Only one form of tax would meet all these criteria, being neither discriminatory, nor opaque nor conducive of profligacy: a Local Sales Tax (LST).

Local Sales Tax

The centrepiece of our reforms to local government is the proposal to scrap VAT and replace it with an LST, to be applied at a county or metropolitan level. Serendipitously, the Treasury happens to raise almost exactly the same amount through VAT (£83.7 billion in 2008-09) as it hands over to local councils in grants (£83 billion). So devolving the power to tax goods and services to town halls would not be an additional levy; rather it would replace an existing and highly unpopular tax.

Unlike VAT, which is complicated and expensive to administer, the LST would be charged just once, at the point of retail. It would be set at the level of a county or metropolitan authority, to avoid the distortions that arise from having concentrations of shops in small localities. Local councils would be free to vary the rate according to their spending needs.

A similar scheme in the United States has given rise to something almost unknown in Britain – tax competition, leading to a downward pressure on rates. State governments are conscious that, if they impose swingeing levies on their retailers, shoppers will cross the state line, followed by whole businesses, thus leading to state bankruptcy and the eviction of the state government by the voters. Opponents of the scheme might object that US states are larger than British counties, and therefore more viable units. In terms of population, this is by no means the case: several British counties have more residents than several US states: Kent, for example, would be the thirty-third most populous state in the Union. To the extent that it is true geographically, the size disparity is an added advantage, giving the British consumer more choice than the American. Such a reform promises substantial benefits.

1. Democratic accountability

Without any Standard Spending Assessment or ring-fenced grants, many of the levers of central control would simply no longer exist. Councillors would have to stand on the basis of their records, and voters would be free to judge them accordingly. A different kind of candidate would soon emerge. In countries where there is a healthy measure of local democracy, it is not uncommon to see local administration in the hands of talented people in their twenties and thirties, running budgets and taking executive decisions as a prelude to careers in national politics.

2. *Fairness*

Unlike other systems of taxation, the LST would affect everyone, to the extent that we all buy things. It correlates closely to disposable wealth, since richer people tend to spend more. But there would be few freeloaders voting for higher spending. The electorate, in other words, would equate closely to the tax base.

3. *Visibility*

At present, local residents don't really know who is responsible for determining local tax bills. Town halls blame Whitehall, Whitehall blames local authorities, and amid all the confusion, local taxes keep rising. With a local sales tax, consumers and voters would see how much they were being charged.

4. *Fiscal probity*

City and county halls would be in direct competition with their neighbours. Set the rate too high and retail sales might slump. Set the rate too low and the boost to retail sales might not be enough to avoid a fall in revenues. Far from being a disadvantage, this competition would be enormously beneficial, for it would force local councils to accept the logic of the 'Laffer Curve': that is, that setting lower tax rates might net them greater revenues. Moreover, business and trade might well be attracted to low-tax areas, broadening the tax base and reinforcing that outcome.

5. *Lower taxes*

As a starting point, we would expect local authorities to set local sales tax rates at an average of roughly 17.5 per cent, the current level of VAT. However, the rate could vary considerably. Some authorities might choose to set a higher rate in the hope of raising more money for better local services; others may tolerate service cuts in order to keep the rate down. Either way, there would be a strong element of competition between different tax jurisdictions. The relentless growth of government might finally be checked.

6. Freedom to scrap council tax

In keeping with the principles of pluralism and local autonomy, councils should be allowed to raise the remaining 25 per cent of their budgets by whatever means their electorates approve. The existence of the LST as the main source of local income would ensure that they would be held to account by the electorate as a whole, and could not impose arbitrary or punitive duties on a minority. Among the available options for additional top-up revenue would be fees and charges for services, a local income tax, a property-based levy, a local business rate or – for the most frugal – nothing at all.

Local decision-making

Fiscal autonomy is only a beginning. Local councils should also be given genuine power over issues of essentially local concern. To start with, almost all of the functions currently exercised by the Department of Communities and Local Government could and should be devolved. Of immense concern to most voters, albeit understandably ignored by national media, are what one might call local quality-of-life issues: the siting of mobile phone masts, the building of incinerators, the crowding-together of new houses. Being necessarily local issues, they tend to be missed by commentators during general election campaigns. Yet they leave people feeling outraged, not only because of the immediate impact on their communities, but because of their sense of powerlessness. It is bad enough that someone should want to build a tower block at the end of your road, but it is maddening to be told that his authority has come from Whitehall, on the advice of a local Regional Authority, and that, however you vote, you cannot influence the outcome. Planning decisions – except in the case of projects of strategic national importance, such as major airports – should be transferred to local authorities.

The benefit of such localisation would soon be seen in voters' attitudes as well as in public administration. Making elected representatives responsible for the consequences of their actions will tend also to make their voters more responsible in their approach.

Which other powers should be devolved? The one great example of devolution from Westminster, the 1998 Scotland Act, sets a precedent. All the fields of policy currently within the purview of the Holyrood Parliament should be transferred to English counties and cities (thereby, incidentally, answering the West Lothian Question). We would also go further and make county and metropolitan authorities responsible for social security. Whether or not there was a parallel process of devolution from Edinburgh to Scottish local authorities – or, indeed, to revived Scottish counties – would be a matter for Scottish voters.

Every survey by the National Audit Office indicates that local councils are less inefficient than Whitehall ministries. Yet power continues to be centralised, in defiance of public opinion, good governance and common sense. Reversing that current of power is the single best thing a new government could do.

6. Putting patients in control

➤ Allow patients to opt out of the NHS and instead pay their contributions into individual health accounts

➤ A proportion of these accounts to be used for everyday healthcare, and a proportion set aside for insurance against serious illness

➤ Government to continue to pay the cover of those who choose to remain within the system, or who cannot afford to create individual accounts

➤ Incentivisation of prevention rather than cure

The national sickness service

Sixty years after its foundation, does anyone still believe that the NHS is 'the envy of the world'? The NHS compares poorly with every alternative system in states of comparable wealth. Barack Obama may be promising universal healthcare in the US, but he would not dream of implementing a system like Britain's.

Report after report finds the NHS wanting. One, published by Eurocare in 2007, found that Britain has one of the worst cancer survival rates in Europe, and was very far behind the best in the study, the United States. England has a female cancer survival rate of only 52.7 per cent, compared with 62.9 per cent for the United States or 61.8 per cent for Iceland. Britain performed worse than former Communist countries such as Slovenia, not to mention Spain and Malta. Men in England had a survival rate of only 44.8 per cent compared with the United States at 66.3 per cent. Another report in the *British Medical Journal* concluded that Britain has some of the poorest stroke treatment rates in Europe.

Before addressing the problem posed by Britain's health system, the first step is to acknowledge it. Alcoholics Anonymous-style, we must admit that the NHS, as it is currently constituted, is failing. We must first diagnose the problem and then prescribe a proportionate remedy. It will not do to accuse any reformers of seeking to 'Americanise the NHS', nor to keep repeating 'Free At The Point Of Use' as a political slogan, a way to shut down any

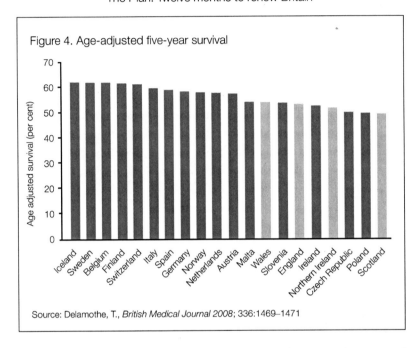

Figure 4. Age-adjusted five-year survival

Source: Delamothe, T., *British Medical Journal 2008*; 336:1469–1471

argument. Most Western healthcare systems provide universal cover, and most are far kinder to the poor than is the NHS.

The NHS is one among many institutions that make up the quango state. Like other bureaucracies, it contains many devoted, selfless and brilliant people; yet, institutionally, it tends to give too much weight to producers, too little to consumers.

Nor should we be shy of pointing out that it is expensive. True, it is not as expensive as it might be. Several insurance-based European healthcare systems, while they deliver better outcomes than the NHS, absorb substantially higher proportions of national spending. It could be argued that, given this disparity, the NHS does not do so badly. But this is to ignore the chief cause of its cheapness: its ability to exploit its position as a near-monopoly employer. It has always been curious that some of the fiercest resistance to any modernisation of Britain's healthcare has come from the public sector unions whose members would be the chief beneficiaries of such modernisation.

The NHS is so structured as to give patients no incentive to shop around for value when seeking treatment. Costs are thereby artificially inflated,

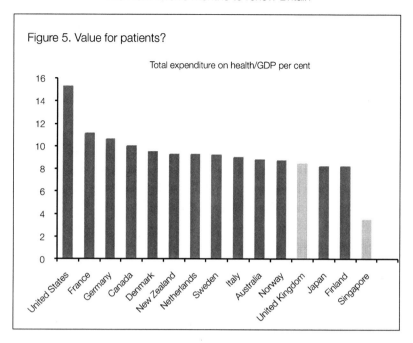

Figure 5. Value for patients?

Total expenditure on health/GDP per cent

meaning that there is less to go around for everyone else. That this criticism applies equally to insurance-based systems does not make it any less valid.

There are people who find the very mention of money in the context of healthcare distasteful. Surely there is something elevated and ennobling about knowing that the sick will be cured regardless of their means, they say. Health, after all, is a universal human need. (So, even more, is food, although no one argues that it should be apportioned by a National Food Service.)

Fair enough. If you are squeamish about considerations of economy, think instead about considerations of lifestyle. It is often pointed out that the NHS would be better named the 'National Sickness Service', since its function is to treat maladies that have already developed rather than anticipate them. True. But the logical inference is rarely drawn. If there were some price mechanism in healthcare, people might make more effort to avoid developing conditions that require expensive cures. In July 2008, the Government calculated that it was spending £750 million a year on drugs to treat preventable conditions. The NHS is spending a million pounds a week on anti-obesity drugs alone. Is this really better than a system which might encourage people to eat more healthily and take exercise?

In any case, if the last ten years have taught us anything about healthcare, it is surely that spending more money does not guarantee better results. Labour increased spending by an extraordinary £43 billion in five years, and then slowed the rate of investment only slightly. But a report by the Office for National Statistics in April 2008 showed that productivity had fallen by 10 per cent over the previous ten years. In some cases, the extra spending had not been useless, but actively harmful: the new GP contracts, for example, encouraged many doctors, perfectly rationally, to work shorter hours.

Healthier alternatives

So, if not the NHS, what? Which countries do better? The United States is often said to have a market-based healthcare system. Does it have anything to teach us?

US healthcare is nothing like as bad as is sometimes believed in Europe. It is a myth, for example, that it does not provide for the poor. The US government spends more per capita on healthcare than any major European government apart from Germany. A far more serious objection is the sheer cost of US healthcare: 16 per cent of GDP. The US system is burdened by too much litigation, regulation and producer capture. We can do better.

So how about Europe? While there are several models of healthcare on the Continent, most of them tend to involve a mixture of private and state provision and to be founded on health insurance. Insurance-based systems are demonstrably better than the NHS, but they, too, are expensive. Defenders of the NHS claim that the expenditure on the Continent is the only reason why the NHS performs so badly in comparison. Actually, we do not need to look across the Channel to see that there is no simple correlation between spending and outcomes: the NHS in Scotland performs worse than that in England on almost every measure, despite considerably higher spending (£2,313 per head in the former compared with £1,915 in the latter in 2006–07).

A system seldom looked at is that of Singapore, a wealthy, developed, Commonwealth nation. Singapore boasts health outcomes that surpass those of many European nations, yet spends only 3.5 per cent of GDP on health compared with Britain's 8.4 per cent.

Singapore operates a system of health savings accounts which puts ultimate power in the hands of doctors and patients. Instead of relying on a government-funded or insurance-based scheme, Singaporeans save money in accounts dedicated for personal healthcare. Combined with low-cost catastrophic insurance cover, health expenditure is managed by the individual in association with his or her doctor. This avoids the rationing and waiting lists intrinsic in the NHS, as well as the bureaucracy characteristic of insurance-based systems. Of course, the state acts as a safety net for those unable to save enough to meet their heath needs, but most people are able to manage their health needs without the government. The Singaporean government pays for only 31 per cent of health expenditure.

When people need treatment, they go directly to the healthcare provider they wish to see. They pay for this treatment from their savings accounts. In the event of catastrophic illness that would overwhelm a savings account, the insurance system pays the bill. Catastrophic insurance differs from traditional health insurance in that it is not accessed every time you see a medical professional. Catastrophic insurance is seldom, if ever, activated, so premiums are kept low.

Once Singaporeans have enough in their savings accounts to meet future expected needs, they no longer have to pay into their account and so have an incentive not to overspend. Because Singaporeans benefit if they moderate their health spending, they are cost-conscious and will shop around for a medical provider who offers good value for money. This price sensitivity reduces health costs more effectively than rationing agencies such as the UK's National Institute for Health and Clinical Evidence (NICE).

Amazingly, Singapore provides this great health system with fewer doctors, nurses and bureaucrats per capita than most developed nations, suggesting an efficiency that is lacking in centrally-planned or insurance-based models. This is a health system for patients, not doctors' unions.

The difference between foreseeable costs and insurance
Private insurance is often cited as an alternative to the NHS, but this is the wrong approach. A sad reality of life is that most of us will get old,

be very ill for a few years and die. As Shakespeare observes, the readiness is all.

Insuring against such illnesses is like insuring a vintage Jaguar against a breakdown. Insurance companies know that humans, like Jaguar cars, are extremely likely to break down – resulting in extremely high insurance premiums. Like insuring a car for theft or accident, we should insure ourselves for only catastrophic illnesses. As Jaguar owners save for repairs or replacements, humans should save for the expected illnesses.

A key component of Singapore's success is the introduction of price sensitivity into the health market. When funded by insurance or a state healthcare system, individuals have no interest in the cost of treatment. They have been paying for it in taxes or insurance premiums and now seek to maximise their benefit. Patients demand and often receive the most expensive care over a cheaper option, often for little or no gain in outcome. No insurance company or government can draft guidelines to cover every clinical eventuality and discretion is left to the clinician, who also lacks any incentive to restrain costs.

With savings accounts, a patient with high cholesterol is likely to adopt a healthier lifestyle and diet rather than consume expensive statins. With patients suddenly price sensitive, health providers will be under pressure to offer their services in a far more cost-effective manner. A patient offered two solutions to an illness, one with 5 per cent better outcomes for twice the price, may choose the cheaper option. British people have been conditioned over the years to be aghast at the thought of pricing safety, but this is a trade-off we already make in every other field of life.

Think of, say, buying a car. If we spent our money on nothing else, many could afford to purchase a brand-new Volvo with all the safety features. The reality is that most of us do not. Such decisions in healthcare are already made, though not by the individual, but by the government – many of the latest treatments are denied to patients because they do not fit a cost-benefit analysis.

Or think of it another way. The demand for healthcare is unlimited. As life expectancy improves, the phenomenon of diminishing returns becomes inescapable: we could, in theory, spend gargantuan sums to prolong our lives for a few hours. Doing so within the existing model means depriving others of the resources, and puts those who must make the decision in the dreadful situation of trying to place a value on life. Never mind efficacy: it is morally better that people who can afford to make a contribution should make their own choices.

Giving patients such freedom will, of course, make the healthcare system more innovative and quicker to adapt, so greatly improving the prospects of everyone, including those who cannot make provision for themselves and must look to the state.

Technology is changing rapidly. In areas such as mobile phones, consumer electronics and computing, new innovations are quickly introduced into the market, yet such innovations are slow in the NHS. The NHS in Scotland recently only received the latest CT scanner because of sponsorship from the Royal Bank of Scotland. With a health system freed from bureaucracy we can only speculate at the innovations likely to occur.

With the shifting of health off the government books, efficiency in the health system ceases to be about savings for the Exchequer. Cost effectiveness in a reformed system is about leaving more for us to spend on our own healthcare.

A system of health savings accounts would remove power from the health administrators and hand real power to the patient. Any system which disconnects the consumer from the cost consequences of their decisions requires a bureaucracy to ensure that the consumer (patient) does not consume too much. Note here that we are not resorting to the trite call of putting doctors in charge of the health system. The British Medical Association may like doctors to be in control but, for all the reasons set out in Part One, we should not let 'experts' invigilate their own professions. Doctors are not the most important individuals in the health service: patients are. Putting patients in charge of their own healthcare, advised by medical professionals, is advanced localism.

We believe that such a system could be quickly phased in by way of a voluntary opt-in structure. It would permit those who wish to use the new system to do so, while allowing others to remain in the NHS. For a while Britain may have two health systems, but through this competition we will be able to judge the success or failure of the two models.

Such a system would involve individuals initially paying around ten per cent of their income into their health account. This would be offset by a compensating tax cut. From this payment, a small amount (£300 to £400 per annum) would be used to pay for private catastrophic medical insurance.

Individual citizens would choose the health services they wanted. If they chose to see their GP, they would pay whatever rate they and the GP agreed. If they wished to see a GP after hours, they could do so: there might be a higher fee, but that would be between them and the GP. If they thought that an ailment required a specialist, they could go directly to a specialist of their choice, bypassing the GP.

Restraining individuals' spending would be in the knowledge that if they achieved a certain balance, they would cease to have to pay into their (interest bearing) savings accounts. These targets would have to be refined over time, but based on current levels of expenditure we estimate that the following targets would be prudent.

Figure 6: How much will we need?

Time from retirement*	Savings target
Upon retirement (R)	£80,000
R – 10 years	£60,000
R – 20 years	£40,000
R – 30 years	£20,000
R – 40 years	£1,000

An important part of this concept is that 80 per cent of health expenditure occurs in the last two years of life, hence the importance to build up savings before retirement. A key challenge for the implementation of such a policy is how to handle a person joining the scheme at ten years before retirement. Such an individual would have no savings and a target of £60,000 that they would be unlikely to achieve in the ten years remaining. Borrowing from the experience of Chilean pension reforms, a government bond, equivalent to the target less £10,000, would be issued and deposited into a savings account.

This takes an opaque unfunded government liability (the amount the government expects to pay for your future healthcare) and makes it a transparently funded liability. This transfer is fiscally neutral, and may in fact benefit the Exchequer by retaining an incentive for an individual to save.

This is not a shift to a non-universal scheme. We are committed to a system that covers all citizens, whatever their circumstances. Most people might be able to look after their healthcare, free from government targets and bureaucracies. But some will never manage to earn enough to pay enough into their own savings or catastrophic insurance accounts. Here the state must continue funding healthcare through the welfare system, and there will need to be state oversight ensuring that expenditure is required and cost effective. The poorest will receive a better quality of care than now, partly due to market efficiencies which will make the entire health sector more competitive, but also because instead of attempting to look after all citizens the government is focusing on the most vulnerable.

Singapore: better results at less than half the price
Other aspects of the Singaporean system worth imitating include the ability to borrow against the health savings account for low-risk investments, especially house purchases; making health accounts bequeathable; and, within certain limits, making them transferable to family members or others who need help.

The health savings accounts system outlined here offers a solution that will create a better, more cost-effective system that remains universal and is available to all, regardless of their state of health and income. Health savings accounts will deliver the sort of service the NHS cannot begin to approach. They will do so by freeing the individual, allowing innovation and making the system accountable in a way that a centralised bureaucracy cannot. If our aim is to improve the healthcare of the poorest, this is the best way to achieve this goal.

7. Neighbourhood welfare

➤ Return responsibility for the relief of poverty to local government
➤ Allow counties and cities to determine eligibility for benefits
➤ Initially, allocate the funds for social security to councils as a bloc grant, with local discretion over their allocation, but move in time to fiscal autonomy
➤ Facilitate the disbursement of benefits by local non-state agents

In Britain as in most of the developed world, welfare spending is rising without any appreciable impact on either poverty or inequality. The bill for social security benefits and tax credits has increased by £35.5 billion since 1993, and now exceeds £140 billion a year. If this sum were simply parcelled out among the poorest 25 per cent of people in Britain, they would become moderately well-off, with a household income considerably higher than the mean working wage. But, of course, this does not happen: the money now goes on sustaining a massive apparatus whose priority is its own survival.

Britain is not alone. For more than half a century, Western countries – with one notable exception – have watched their social security budgets balloon with little appreciable effect on either relative or absolute poverty. Benefits which were intended as one-off and transformative have instead become permanent, as recipients arrange their affairs around qualifying for subventions. Millions have become trapped in the squalor of disincentives and low expectations. Western governments have proved that, as long as you pay people to be poor, you will never run out of poor people.

The exception is the United States which, in 1996, thoroughly overhauled its welfare system. On every measurable indicator, the reforms have been a triumphant success. Poverty, unemployment and welfare budgets have fallen sharply, while satisfaction among former benefits claimants has soared.

It is true that the 1996 Act was passed at a time of strong economic growth; but this alone does not explain the almost miraculous shift from dependency to gainful work. The number of families on welfare has fallen from 5 million to 2 million. There are 1.6 million fewer children in poverty. And, perhaps most impressive, the reforms lifted groups who had been untouched by every previous welfare initiative: poverty among black children fell from 42 to 33 per cent; among single mothers from 50 to 42 per cent.

So what was the magical formula? What wand did President Clinton – or, if you prefer, Newt Gingrich and his fellow Congressmen – wave to conjure so extraordinary a transformation? Essentially, they devolved responsibility. The chief purpose of the 1996 Personal Responsibility and Work Opportunity Act was to shift social security from the federal government to the states, and to give local authorities incentives to reduce their caseloads. Offered the freedom to experiment, the states seized it with gusto. Some incentivised employers to take on the workless; others organised schemes themselves; most made the receipt of benefits conditional on taking up job offers. Best practice quickly spread, as states copied what worked elsewhere.

At the same time, no state could afford to carry on as before, signing cheques with a minimum of questions asked. Doing so would, as legislators understood well, make such a state a magnet for every bum in America. There was, in short, a measure of healthy competition.

Could something similar work in Britain? Absolutely. The relief of poverty was seen as a municipal responsibility – indeed, the chief municipal responsibility – for hundreds of years prior to the 1911 Liberal reforms. Most legislation, from Tudor times onwards, was concerned with enforcing localism: in other words, with keeping welfare claimants in parishes where they were known. The rationale of the vagrancy laws was two-fold. First, that local authorities were best placed to distinguish between deserving and undeserving cases: it was feared that 'sturdy beggars' would pass themselves off as genuinely needy where they were unknown. Second, that it was morally better for taxpayers to alleviate poverty in their own communities: to discharge their duty to their immediate neighbours, rather than to 'the poor' in general.

These considerations ought also to apply today. As things stand, we have an anomalous system whereby county councils and metropolitan authorities are responsible for the delivery of social services, but have no say over the policies which they are charged with implementing. They are obliged to pay benefits, but have no discretion over who qualifies for them.

A simple administrative reform would allow local authorities to determine entitlement levels (although, ideally, such a reform would come as part of the much wider shift towards self-financing councils set out earlier). Several British counties and cities have larger populations than several US states. And the most successful US states, notably Florida and Wisconsin, were the ones that devolved responsibility further, to local welfare boards and county authorities. British councils already have the staff in place to run social security. All they lack are concrete incentives to ameliorate the system.

The advantages of localism in welfare are easily listed.

1. Large bureaucracies create unintended consequences.
Whereas councils can tailor their policies to suit local needs, a uniform system that covers 60 million people is bound to contain loopholes, tempting into dependency some who were never envisaged as claimants.

2. Proximity facilitates discernment.
Person A may be a deserving widow who has been unlucky, while person B is a known layabout. Local caseworkers may see this clearly. But if the universal rules handed down from Whitehall place the two applicants in the same category, they must be treated identically.

3. Pluralism spreads best practice.
The freedom to innovate means that local authorities will come up with ideas and pilot schemes that the Department of Social Security would never have dreamed of. Those that work will be copied elsewhere so that, as in the US, councillors start speaking of 'adopting the Surrey model' or 'introducing Essex-style reforms'.

4. Immediacy encourages involvement.
Non-state agents – churches, charities, businesses – are more likely to involve themselves in local projects than in national schemes. Such organisations are far better at taking people out of poverty than are government agencies.

5. Localism transforms attitudes.

At present, many see benefit fraud as cheating 'the system' rather than cheating their neighbours. A recent advertising campaign in North East England aimed at stigmatising bogus claims had the effect of increasing fraud, by showing people how easy it was. We would take a very different attitude towards, say, the neighbour whom we knew to be claiming incapacity benefit while working as an electrician, if we felt the impact in our local tax bill.

6. Autonomy favours frugality.

At present, high-spending local councils have a perverse incentive to increase welfare dependency, and thereby swell the proportion of the local electorate beholden to high-spending parties. Several Labour authorities employ officials whose job it is to encourage take-up of entitlements of which local people might have been unaware. The rationale is that, since the benefits are paid by central government, more money is thereby attracted to the area. And so more people are trapped by the low calculation of their local politicians.

7. Localism restores responsibility.

This is potentially the greatest advantage of all, for localism should encourage greater responsibility in every sense: our responsibility to support ourselves if we can, but also our responsibility to those around us – not an abstract category of 'the underprivileged', but visible neighbours – who, for whatever reason, cannot support themselves. No longer would our obligation be discharged when we have paid our taxes. Localism, in short, would make us better citizens.

A closer look at the United States

'Wisconsin' has suddenly become a buzzword in Britain. MPs who would struggle to point out that lake-bounded state on a map, let alone explain its social security reforms, use its name to signify, in rough terms, getting people off welfare and into work. All the main parties are now showing some interest in importing 'Wisconsin', as they understand the word, into Britain.

But it is vital to see Wisconsin's welfare reforms in context. They were chiefly about the devolution of power, not about the imposition of some ready-made formula from the centre. The idea that a social security minister can impose 'Wisconsin' from Whitehall is based on a fundamental misunderstanding of how localism precedes reform.

Opponents of the localisation of welfare in the US, of whom there were many at the time (though they are few now), were frenzied in their criticism. One Democrat decried the 1996 reforms as 'the most brutal act of social policy since Reconstruction'. Many more predicted that it would lead to a spike in poverty and destitution. In fact, as we have seen, the 'race to the bottom' which opponents feared was precisely what made the reform so successful. Competition encouraged states to be active in shifting people off welfare rather than simply administering the system. It is in this context that we should glance at two of the most successful examples.

Wisconsin
Prior to the 1996 welfare reform act, a handful of states developed pilot projects to see if welfare could be improved. Arguably, the most successful was Wisconsin, which became a driving force behind devolving welfare from the federal government to state governments. The Wisconsin story is another example of why welfare should not only be implemented, but also designed, by local government.

Critics forecast that if states were given budgetary autonomy in welfare, they would cut benefits and services in order to drive the impoverished into neighbouring states. However, Wisconsin saw its welfare caseloads drop by almost 70 per cent between 1987 and 1997 while caseloads in the rest of the country rose steeply. By 2004 almost 67 per cent of Wisconsin welfare recipients were working. Wisconsin did not export its unemployed; it spent 45 per cent more per family and found them jobs, self-respect and a sense of personal empowerment.

Wisconsin introduced a set of reforms, including programmes to get most capable welfare claimants off benefits and into the workforce as soon as possible. Under the reform W-2, recipients were individually evaluated to measure their employability. In each category, recipients were held accountable for their performance; if they failed to complete their required activities they were sanctioned. For example, if they failed to show up for work they faced financial penalties. Appeal processes were put into place to protect against abuse of the system by both recipients and caseworkers. Rather than balking at this raised level of responsibility and accountability, a large number of recipients liked the system, reporting increased self-esteem and hopefulness for the future.

Recognising that welfare hurdles lie not just with the recipients but also the bureaucracies, the Wisconsin state reform 'Pay for Performance' held regional offices accountable for their performance. No longer would counties be allocated a set amount of funding for welfare services but they would be required to 'earn' those funds by increasing the number of recipients placed in jobs or community-service work. This regime also introduced competition, opening welfare contracts not just to public services but also private providers. Incentivised under this programme, inner-city Milwaukee caseworkers increased job placements by 30 per cent.

Florida
Perhaps the most dynamic of any of the American welfare reforms, Florida did not merely tweak the former system under its new authority but rather introduced an entirely new social contract for the poor. While the Florida reform reflected major American trends in welfare reform (including time limits on benefits and work requirements), its major contribution to welfare policy was its emphasis on local control and local accountability.

Floridian policy-makers understood that one size doesn't fit all. What works in one part of the state won't work in another. Special considerations need to be given to each of the communities' particular needs. Policies designed to help those in tourism-based economies like Miami won't work for those living in small agricultural towns such as Immokalee. Florida created 24 regional boards, not only to develop their own strategies, but also to execute welfare services in their local regions.

This devolved not only the policy of welfare but also its administration to small local units. The only state-wide requirement was that each region must meet a core set of programme goals. In a testament to benefits of devolution, nearly every region met or exceeded almost every programme goal. Despite fears that the poor would be left behind, those regions that failed to make the goals were put on administrative watch until they improved.

Who learned from whom?

The Americans were not the first to treat poverty locally. Britain traditionally sought to address poverty at the local level. The Poor Law, and associated vagrancy acts, emphasised local management of the poor. Friendly societies were recognised by Parliament in 1793. These societies offered flexible, voluntary welfare programmes that fairly and successfully served manual workers and their families during the industrial revolution. But local welfare was destroyed in 1911 by the National Insurance Act.

Friendly societies were self-governing and self-funding mutual benefit associations created as a safety-net for manual workers. Societies determined how much members should contribute, who should receive benefits and how much they ought to receive. Some provided illness benefits, others did not. They provided an extremely efficient and beneficial social safety net despite the dislocations caused by rapid industrialisation.

Both voluntarism and localism are, as we have seen, alien to the modern ministers, perennially under pressure to 'do something'. These days, ministers seek to reform welfare through Whitehall diktats. In 1997, Labour introduced New Deal programmes aimed at reducing youth unemployment. However, despite economic growth over the past ten years and 2.9 million new jobs, the rate of unemployment of 18- to 24-year-olds is higher than in 1997. At the very least, the New Deal has been a colossal waste of money; arguably it has been worse than useless, inflating the expectations of its graduates, discouraging them from taking jobs that they would previously have accepted, and so being a net cause of unemployment. Such are the unintended and perverse consequences that attend on centralised decision-making.

To give another example, deficiencies in the tax and benefits system generate disincentives to work, and the situation is getting worse thanks to Gordon Brown's reliance on means-testing. According to the Institute for Fiscal Studies:

Changes to income tax, employee National Insurance contributions, council tax, tax credits and benefits alone strengthened work incentives on average under the Conservatives and have weakened them under Labour.

This does not tell the whole story. Gordon Brown's expansion of tax credits focused on households with dependent children; much less generosity was shown to working age households without dependent children. Indeed, among the latter, poverty, as officially defined, is now not only increasing in relative terms, but in absolute terms, too, as the then minister, John Hutton, admitted in the House of Commons in 2007. For this group, worklessness is certainly not being compensated for by earnings-linked increases in means-tested benefits; so what is keeping them out of gainful employment?

A large part of the answer lies in the wide range of personal obstacles experienced by the working age, workless population. These include genuine disabilities and illness, behavioural issues such as substance addiction and a lack of relevant skills and experience to bring to the jobs market. The Government's Welfare Reform Bill was introduced to tackle these issues with the specific objective of reducing the incapacity benefit count – Britain's hidden reserve of long-term unemployed.

Charities, not bureaucracies
The trouble is that the state is bad at achieving its goals. It is especially unsuited to tackling the complex and multiple issues that individuals face in getting back to work. Voluntary organisations are far better suited to the personal approach required to overcome the underlying causes of joblessness. In theory, at least, Labour ministers have at last acknowledged the potential of the voluntary sector in delivering government programmes.

Can we therefore expect a radical decentralisation of the welfare system and a devolution of decision-making power to charities focusing on the needs of the individual? Unfortunately not – because though this government is opening up employment services and other public programmes to providers from outside the public sector, it is simultaneously centralising control over the commissioning of such services. Examples of the new centralisation can be found in the Offender Management Bill and the Freud Report on the Government's welfare to work strategy. The following comment by William Higham of the Prison Reform Trust is typical of the concerns of small charities:

It's one thing to go after a vibrant, mixed economy, it's another to structure it in such a way that only certain people can compete on an even playing field. Regional commissioning is appropriate for some services, but the bulk of work is very local in nature and anything that would risk squeezing out the small charities and community groups has to be guarded against.

Where contracts or grants were once awarded on a local basis, they are being consolidated into much larger area contracts so that the commissioning agency has only a few contractors to deal with. This approach tends to freeze out smaller, locally-based charities – whose strength and expertise derives from the roots they have in particular communities. Moreover, charities of all sizes find themselves disadvantaged by the super-contracting approach because, being charities, they face restrictions on the amount of working capital they can raise – an essential requirement when late-paying, multi-million-pound contracts impose major cashflow issues on the service provider. In other words, Labour is restructuring our public services in such a way that only large private companies have a chance of participating on something like an equal footing to the state. In such circumstances, charities can stay involved only as sub-contractors, a precarious position in which they find themselves dancing to corporate agendas and absorbing the costs of management fees.

The surest way to give charities a greater role is through devolution. Not only are local authorities likelier to turn to organisations prominent in their communities: individuals, businesses and others are more likely to come forward when the initiatives in question are of a local and human scale.

Making people part of a large, headless, impersonal system is not the type of support those who are jobless need to become independent. Turning someone's life around is a nurturing process, something better done on an individual level rather than making the poor cogs in the welfare machine. Putting a face on poverty and tying it into the local community is an empowering method to improve society as a whole.

8. The Great Repeal Bill

➤ Repeal the Acts that provide the legal base for burdensome and costly regulation
➤ Provide a mechanism for continuous repeal
➤ Introduce sunset clauses on new Bills

We still think of Britain as a parliamentary democracy. But, in recent years, that traditional model has been quietly subverted. There has been a shift in power from the legislature to the executive so insidious and colossal that, had it been enacted openly, it would be reckoned a *coup d'état*: an overturning of the parliamentary settlement won in 1689.

The clearest external measure of the revolution is the shift from parliamentary legislation – Bills debated and voted upon by elected representatives – to statutory instruments. A statutory instrument is, essentially, a way for a minister to order change without the trouble of having to alter the law. Often, statutory instruments are used to give effect to EU rules. It is the statutory instrument, rather than primary legislation, that is today the chief mechanism for the regulation of Britain.

Statutory instruments were rare before the 1970s. But they grew rapidly thereafter, largely in response to EU membership. In 1980, there were 2,051, in 1990 2,667, in 2000 3,424. Measured another way, in 2005 – the last year for which figures are available – there were almost 12,000 pages of new statutory instruments. At the same time, naturally enough, the number of Acts of Parliament has declined slightly.

Statutory instruments receive only occasional and cursory parliamentary oversight. Of the 1,380 statutory instruments laid before Parliament as delegated legislation in the 2006–07 session, 12 were considered by the House of Commons itself and only 202 by a committee of the House. Never before has the amount of new regulation been so great, nor the scrutiny of it so limited.

These regulations cost the government little, but the private sector a great deal. The government's own Better Regulation Commission has estimated the total cost of regulation to the UK economy at 10 to 12 per cent of GDP,

116

or £100 billion. All politicians like to talk about 'cutting red tape'. Few have considered how it might be done.

The way to reduce regulation is to scrap the laws that provide its legal basis. Rather than fitfully baling out the tub, we should screw the tap shut. Here, we propose an initial list of laws to be repealed – starting with an Act which neatly manifests what has been wrong with previous efforts at deregulation.

This list is indicative, not exhaustive. Its items came about through a collective effort: what we have previously termed 'wiki-politics'. We posted a blog on the ConservativeHome website, and had hundreds of responses. We should be prepared to add to the Great Repeal Bill on a similar basis, running a website that allowed people and businesses hampered by rules and regulations to post their concerns and to propose their repeal.

1. The Legislative and Regulatory Reform Act

It tells us all we need to know about what is wrong with Whitehall that, in seeking to tackle the problem of excessive red tape, the government's response was not to repeal legislation or close down quangos, but to pass a new law and create a new quango: the Better Regulation Commission.

The Legislative and Regulatory Reform Act was supposed to establish statutory principles of good regulation based on the work of the Commission. Far from solving the problem of excessive regulation – itself caused by an unrestrained executive – the Act allows what amounts to government by executive decree. It empowers ministers to enact statutory instruments to reform legislation that is perceived to be 'outdated, unnecessary or over-complicated'. Ministers can change the law on the recommendation of the unelected Law Commission, but without reference to the body elected to make law, Parliament.

Instead of using new quangos and executive power to sort out the over-regulation caused by overly powerful quangos, the solution lies in doing the opposite. We have already set out our plan to make quango chiefs plead annually before the relevant Commons committees for their continued funding and, indeed, their continued existence. In such an environment, officials would find themselves under far greater pressure not to over-regulate.

2. Statutory rules on dismissal

Since October 2004, an employer dismissing an employee has been legally required to comply with a statutory minimum three-step disciplinary procedure, loading small businesses with significant additional burdens. Even if an employer follows the dismissal procedure to the letter of the law, it is still possible for the dismissal to be judged unfair.

We would repeal the Employment Act 2002 (Chapter 1 of Part 1 of Schedule 2 and paragraphs 6 and 9 of Schedule 2) and the Employment Act 2002 (Dispute Resolution) Regulations 2004 SI 2004/752. Contracts are a matter between employer and employee. If both parties are content, the state has no business coming between them and declaring the contract illegal.

3. Works Council Regulations

The European Works Council Directive came into force on 15 January 2000. It places obligations on employers to consult employees, and in doing so hampers productivity and job creation.

The Great Repeal Bill would exempt all UK-based employers from the EU's Works Council Directive and withdraw Britain from the European Social Chapter.

4. Part-time and temporary worker regulations

In a similar vein, we would scrap all statutory instruments introduced under the EU directives on part-time work, including Part-time Workers (Prevention of Less Favourable Treatment) Regulations 2000 (SI 2000/1551) and 2002 (SI 2002/2035).

Designed to ensure that part-time workers have the same access to pay, pensions, annual leave and training as full-time staff, these rules have seriously damaged the temping industry which used to be the main route from unemployment into work.

5. Weights and Measures Act

Through the Weights and Measures Act 1985, and various secondary legislation, including the Weights and Measures (Packaged Goods)

Regulations 2006 (SI 2006/659), businesses are told in some detail how to package and sell goods.

There is no need for the government to stipulate what measures business uses. Nor is there any evidence that these rules benefit consumers.

6. Home Information Pack regulations

Regulations requiring Home Information Packs introduced in 2006 are unnecessary. At a time when the housing market is slowing down, they add extra transaction costs. Designed to ensure greater energy efficiency, they fail in their primary purpose.

Not only would we scrap the Home Information Pack rules, we would also repeal those sections of the 2004 Housing Act that allowed them to be introduced in the first instance.

7. Operating and financial reviews

The 2005 Statutory Instrument No. 1011 under the Companies Act 1985 places detailed and excessive obligations on companies to produce operating and financial reviews and directors' reports. We would abolish them.

If there is a commercial demand for such reports, companies will produce them.

8. Money laundering rules

Regulation designed to deter terrorists and organised criminals is doing neither. Introduced by EU institutions, the rules hamper businesses and inconvenience everyone – by, for instance, making it difficult for some people to open bank accounts.

We would scrap these rules, including Statutory Instruments 2007 No. 2157, 2007 No. 3299, 2006 No. 308, 2006 No. 1070, 2003 No. 171, 2003 No. 3075, 2001 No. 1819 and 2001 No. 3641.

9. The Health and Safety at Work Act

Excessive health and safety regulation is replacing common sense. It is time to review the volume of rules created under the 1974 Health and Safety at Work Act.

The Act created what is now the Health and Safety Executive. It also allows European Union rules and regulations on health and safety to be created and imposed with little regard to any democratically accountable UK institutions. It should be scrapped.

10. Fire safety rules

The Regulatory Reform (Fire Safety) Order 2005 Statutory Instrument No. 1541 forces small businesses to prepare detailed paperwork for audit and inspection, and allows Fire Authorities to shut business premises without appeal, but does little or nothing to make fires less likely.

11. The Standards Board

The Local Government Act 2000 created Standards Boards to oversee the conduct of locally elected councillors. Deeply undemocratic, this rule means that unelected officials may now suspend democratically elected representatives.

Far from safeguarding local democracy, this measure has ensured that much time and effort has had to be wasted investigating spurious allegations. It has done nothing to restore trust in local government and has further infantilised local democracy.

We would repeal those sections of the 2000 Act that enabled the creation of the Standards Board. The mechanism for removing a local councillor should be the ballot box.

12. Best Value regimes

The Best Value regime was introduced by the 1999 Local Government Act. It does not just impose outcomes on local authorities, but determines how local authorities should reach those outcomes. We would repeal those sections of the 1999 Act that deal with Best Value.

13. Comprehensive Performance Assessment

As with Best Value, the Comprehensive Performance Assessment achieves little, yet costs a great deal. We would abolish it. It should be up to local people to make a judgement as to how effectively their local authority was converting their tax pounds into local services.

14. Regional quangos

There are not only too many quangos in Whitehall, but too many bodies at a regional level. The British Chambers of Commerce estimates that this over governance has added a massive £50 billion of extra regulatory cost to British businesses.

Government Offices of the Regions were created in 1994. They are increasingly the means by which government programmes on regeneration, crime, housing, public health and education are imposed. In 2004/05, they accounted for some £9 billion of expenditure.

Regional Development Agencies were created following the Regional Development Agencies Act 1998, and are supposed to be in charge of economic development and regeneration, promoting business efficiency and competitiveness, creating employment, skills and sustainable development. They fail to do any of these things, and fail at considerable public expense – and with almost zero accountability.

Regional Assemblies were created under the same 1998 Act, and are supposed to have some oversight over similar areas of policy.

It should be up to local government to oversee responsibility for these areas of public policy. The Great Repeal Bill would abolish the entire apparatus of regional administration, abolishing both the Government Offices of the Regions, and repealing the early 1990s legislation and the 1998 Act.

15. Criminal Records Bureau

The 1997 Police Act established the Criminal Records Bureau as an Executive Agency of the Home Office. Its purpose is to conduct criminal record checks on potential employees on behalf of organisations and recruiters.

The rationale of the Act was to ensure enhanced safety for children, young people and vulnerable adults. It has achieved the precise opposite.

Delays in gaining clearance have meant that perfectly suitable people have been unable to provide youngsters with supervision and care. Worse, reliance on CRB checks prevents commonsense assessments being made.

The CRB was criticised for ineffectiveness in late 2003 following the Soham murders trial, when a former caretaker, found guilty of murdering two schoolgirls, was found to have had a criminal record and been suspected of string of offences – yet to have been hired to work in a school.

The need for CRB checks is poisoning civic society. Church outings, school plays and numerous other events have been disrupted because volunteers have been barred from working with young people without being vetted in advance.

Worse, from 2009, the newly created Independent Safeguarding Authority will demand that almost all UK adults who potentially work with children are subject to the same procedure.

16. Identity Cards Act 2006
This Act established a National Identity Register database, and gave legal force for the gradual introduction of a national identity card scheme from 2010. The legislation enables enormous amounts of personal data and information to be added to the database.

The justification for this massive, multi-million-pound scheme is that it will make us safer from terrorists and reduce illegal immigration. There is no evidence that it will achieve either.

17. Countryside and Rights of Way Act 2002
Sections 60 to 62 of this Act require each local authority highway agency to implement a Rights of Way Improvement Plan at least every ten years. This should be a matter entirely for each local authority to determine.

18. Hunting Act 2004
The Hunting Act outlaws hunting with dogs. A seriously flawed piece of legislation, the Act does nothing to improve animal welfare, but much to undermine respect for the law.

19. Regulation of Investigatory Powers Act 2000
This Act gives a legal framework to permit the authorities to snoop and spy on the citizenry. Instead of enabling accountable authorities to use such powers in pursuit of terrorists, the Act allows local authorities and petty officialdom to investigate people for minor offences.

The Act creates a quango – the Surveillance Commission – which is supposed to oversee the way authorities use their powers.

The Act has led to an explosion in spying. It should not be unlawful to intercept or collect data about a private citizen without the explicit approval of a magistrate.

20. Police and Criminal Evidence Act 1984

The Police and Criminal Evidence Act 1984 was intended to establish a balance between the powers of the police and the rights of the public. Instead, the Act means officers have to engage in laborious and time-consuming form-filling each time they stop or question someone. This not only ties up police time and resources, but deters police from acting in ways that common sense dictates.

We have already set out proposals to make local police locally accountable. With local democratic oversight, the police would be held to account by local communities.

21. Gambling Act 2005

The Gambling Act 2005 covered everything from 'super casinos' to online gambling. It created a quango – the Gambling Commission – to oversee the industry and regulate it. The Act aimed to control all forms of gambling. It set out to prevent gambling from 'being a source of crime and disorder'. Apart from tackling something that was never a significant problem, it has ended up forcing people to apply for licenses to hold raffles to raise money for church fêtes. Thanks to the tide of regulation that has followed the Act, seaside amusement arcades have had to construct elaborate partitions between different kinds of gaming machines, and comply with rules that no one with internet access has to adhere to.

The Act should be repealed, allowing the gaming industry to revert to the pre-2005 regulatory system. Scrapping the Act would make it easier and cheaper for charities to benefit from fundraising raffles. Pubs would be allowed to hold bingo games for charity without needing an expensive licence.

22. *The Dangerous Dogs Act 1989*
Frequently cited as an example of hasty, ill-considered and knee-jerk legislation, the Dangerous Dogs Act is still on the statute book.

23. *The Football Spectators Act 1989*
A similarly tabloid-driven law from the same period, still absurdly in force.

24. *The War Crimes Act 1991*
Intended to bring old Nazis to trial, the War Crimes Act has not resulted in a single prosecution, but has introduced the notion of retroactive law into British statute.

25. *The Firearms Act 1998*
Passed in the aftermath of the Dunblane tragedy, when emotions were running high, the Act has done nothing to reduce gun crime, although it has criminalised the Olympic sport of pistol shooting.

26. *The European Communities Act 1972*
The 1972 European Communities Act ended centuries of parliamentary sovereignty. Sections (2) and (3) create a mechanism for foreign laws to have direct jurisdiction in Britain without any implementing decision by Parliament. We would repeal those two sections, so that EU Directives and Regulations would be treated as advisory pending a specific Act of Parliament. This would, of course, necessitate a renegotiation of our relationship with the EU. We see such a renegotiation as part of a wider realignment of Britain's foreign policy, to which we now turn.

9. An independent Britain

➤ Scrap Crown Prerogative powers, and subject foreign policy to parliamentary control
➤ Hold committee hearings for senior diplomatic postings
➤ Submit international treaties for re-ratification by the House of Commons
➤ Replace the existing terms of EU membership with a Swiss-style bilateral free-trade agreement
➤ Axe the Defence Industrial Strategy

British foreign policy is cocooned from the democratic process. It is conducted by highly qualified officials who, although often technically brilliant, have drifted away from the values of the rest of the country. There are few mechanisms to make the conduct of diplomatic relations subject to popular scrutiny; in consequence, the state machine is even less subject to democratic control in the field of international affairs than in domestic matters.

Left to their own devices, diplomatists have evolved an approach to international relations that is elitist, managerialist, supra-nationalist, technocratic and contemptuous of 'populism'. Sometimes, this happens to be what is needed. Often, it has ruinous consequences. But, right or wrong, there is precious little that the rest of us can do about it.

Democratising diplomacy
Throughout this book, we have tried to cleave consistently to the principles that power should be dispersed and decision-makers held accountable. Are these general precepts applicable to the field of foreign affairs? Absolutely. Although we rarely think of it as such, the Foreign and Commonwealth Office is simply one among many government *apparats*. Like all state bureaucracies, it will become better at what it does to the extent that it is directly answerable to the rest of us. And, like all state bureaucracies, it will fiercely resist this argument, insisting that the 'experts' should be allowed to get on with their business unmolested by crowd-pleasing demagogues.

The idea of removing a field of policy from political calculations has a superficial attractiveness. The trouble is that, as we have already seen, there is no such thing as an 'expert': the professional is more likely to be biased than the generalist (i.e. the elected minister). The notion that administration works best with minimal democratic control – which is what we mean when we say 'this shouldn't be treated as a political football' – has been the justification of every tyranny in history, from Bonaparte's onwards.

It may be argued that diplomacy is different. It is, after all, a highly specialised field, remote from the everyday concerns of most voters. Its practitioners have evolved particular skills, and a familiarity with their subject that few laymen can match. Yet precisely the same can be argued, *mutatis mutandis*, about policing, education or virtually any other field of government activity.

With little direct oversight, our diplomats have often pursued policies that are not only at odds with popular opinion, but calamitous in their own terms. Think, for example, of the backing that Britain has given to murderous tyrants such as Nicolae Ceausescu, Idi Amin and Robert Mugabe, in the belief that they would turn out to be our friends. Or of our repeated attempts to talk Tehran's ayatollahs out of their nuclear ambitions by being 'constructive'. Or of the spectacular failure of intelligence prior to Argentina's seizure of the Falkland Islands. Or of the alienation of once friendly colonies (a special mention should be made here of Malta which, in 1956, voted by 74 per cent in a referendum for complete integration with the UK; its application was rejected so high-handedly that, within eight years, Malta was completely independent and pursuing an anti-British foreign policy). Think of the appalling mistakes that were made by John Major's Government – in so far as he was able to pursue a policy independent from the UN and the EU – in Yugoslavia. Think, above all, of the FCO's determination always and everywhere to pursue closer European integration.

Many, perhaps most, of these mistakes, might have been avoided had foreign affairs more closely reflected the layman's views. You do not need to a degree in Arabic and Persian studies to see that there is nothing to be gained by cosying up to the current Iranian regime. You do not need to have spent two years at the College of Europe in Bruges to understand why the EU is inimical to British traditions. On the contrary, an excessive specialisation in these fields can impair your vision of Britain's true interests.

All organisations make mistakes, of course, and it is easy to criticise with hindsight. But the conduct of British foreign policy shows certain institutional flaws. To the extent that these failures derive from the way it is structured, they ought to be remediable. It is to these institutional flaws that we now turn.

Why the Foreign Office gets things wrong

Everyone who has been involved with local or national politics is aware of the phenomenon of 'officer control': the tendency of permanent functionaries to run things according to their own convenience and priorities, with minimal input from the elected representatives who are notionally in charge, but who are, in practice, often too busy with their electoral activities to pay much attention to administration.

Certain features are common to almost all bureaucracies. They tend to be risk-averse and reactive. Those who rise to run them generally do so by never sticking their necks out, and by reflecting whatever is the prevailing wisdom of the moment. In consequence, they often cling to once-fashionable theories long after their utility has passed. At the same time, many officials feel bound to one another by the common nexus of their expertise. They dislike being told what to do by those who, as they see it, have no qualification in the field. They are hyper-sensitive to press criticism. They resent what they call 'populism' – which, when you think about it, is what the rest of us call 'democracy'.

All these features can be found, to some extent, in the FCO. A brief survey of the conduct of British foreign policy reveals three particular traits. Our diplomats are *hidebound*, acting according to strategic assumptions that are sometimes decades old. They are *elitist*, their disdain for public opinion at home being matched by a willingness to do business with despots abroad. And they are *supra-nationalist*, both in their fondness for establishing cross-border bureaucracies and in their dislike of secessionist or national movements. These tendencies are worth considering in more detail.

Stuck in the Cold War

Generals, as the old chestnut has it, are always gearing up to fight the last war. Rarely has this been truer than now. Nineteen years after the fall of the Berlin Wall, Britain's deployment and procurement patterns remain trapped in the Cold War. Our largest overseas garrison is not in Iraq or Afghanistan, but in Germany: arguably the most otiose deployment in the history of the British Army. The single largest item of our defence spending has been the Euro-fighter: an aircraft designed to dogfight Soviet MiGs. The naval budget is largely consumed by submarines, whose chief purpose is to keep open the North Atlantic sea lanes.

Meanwhile, we have invested far too little in the modern hardware suited to out-of-area campaigns: air- and sea-lift capacity, guided missile systems, advanced satellites and military computers, unmanned sea-vessels and aircraft, drones.

Our defence budget is not small: at £32 billion a year, it is the world's second-largest, in absolute terms, after that of the United States. The trouble is that much of this sum is spent in the interests of our defence contractors rather than our soldiers. Precisely because there is weak democratic oversight, sophisticated lobbying can ensure that major procurement decisions are skewed, and that cheaper, better and readier alternatives are passed over.

These criticisms ought, of course, to be directed primarily at the Ministry of Defence rather than the FCO. But the misallocation of our defence budget reflects a wider failure to have moved with the times. Our strategic thinking – and, indeed, our diplomatic alignment more generally – remains Euro-centric. It is true that, during the second half of the twentieth century, Britain's interests depended chiefly on the security of Western Europe. But, in the broad sweep of history, this was an extremely unusual period.

What is NATO for?

The end of the Cold War ought to have returned Britain to its traditional role as a global and maritime nation. Our enemies these days are distant and sparse: Iraqi insurgents, Afghan badmashes, West African teenagers. Yet we are fighting them with weapons, structures and alliances designed to defend West Germany against a massed assault by Russian T72s. Instead of determining our security needs and then furnishing ourselves with the *matériel* and institutions best suited to them, we took what we happened already to have – NATO – and tried to press it to a purpose for which it had never been designed.

This is how bureaucracies always behave, of course. No apparatus will ever volunteer to have its role reduced. Rather, it will cast around for a new task to justify itself. Institutional aggrandisement is allied to general inertia. Thus, for example, almost everyone over a certain age will insist that NATO must remain the centrepiece of our defence, without quite being able to explain why.

NATO does, of course, serve many useful purposes. Its members share common values, and it is an important guarantor of a continuing US presence outside the Western hemisphere. But, looked at from first principles, it surely cannot be as central to Britain's interests as it was during the Cold War. The United Kingdom ought to be developing ties with friendly governments on every continent. It should pick key strategic partners in each region in which it has interests. Europe is now just one continent among many. Yet our strategic thinking remains stuck in the 1980s. We are suffering unnecessary casualties in Afghanistan because we are short of helicopters. At the same time, we are spending almost unbelievable sums on Cold War weapons systems. The Euro-fighter and the Trident replacement will cost around £20 billion each. Neither can be usefully deployed against the paramilitary enemies we now face.

Absence of a unifying theory

The real problem is the absence of an overall strategic vision. In the days when the diplomatic service was small, and under direct ministerial control, such vision existed. At the peak of the British Empire, Lord Salisbury directed 52 permanent staff in London, and a handful of ambassadors overseas. Throughout the nineteenth century, Britain had clearly understood international interests: the need to maintain a naval presence in key theatres; the security of the sea-route to India; the spread of free trade; the balance of power in Europe; sympathy for national movements in Europe provided they did not threaten the balance of power; and, later, the two-power naval standard. In those days, Britain combined military power with a wariness of foreign entanglements: it was strong but isolationist. These days, for no very good reason, we are doing the opposite: committing troops all over the world without committing the necessary resources to raise them.

Part of the reason for our confusion is that, unlike in Salisbury's day, there is little holistic understanding of Britain's strategic needs. The policies listed above followed naturally from an analysis of Britain's interests as a mercantile island nation. Today, the FCO's official statement of our strategic goals, *Active Diplomacy in a Changing World*, is comprised of nine unrelated and almost random objectives. In the absence of an overall strategic vision, our policy has become reactive, hand-to-mouth. We default automatically to whatever happens to be in place, rather than thinking about what we should ideally like.

This is partly the 'sunk costs' phenomenon, which is by no means peculiar to British diplomacy. But it can lead to some terrible mistakes. We backed Idi Amin until well into the 1970s, and Robert Mugabe until well into the 1990s, because we felt we had invested so much in them. We supported the Shah of Iran for the same reason, with catastrophic consequences. We are now repeating the mistake in Saudi Arabia. At no stage have we defined, from first principles, what kind of world we want, and who our friends are in such a world, and then reassessed our priorities accordingly.

Our support for various authoritarian regimes is not just a symptom of inertia. Something more unlovely is also at work.

'People like us'

Look at the parts of the world where Washington's interests clash most directly with those of Brussels. These may be grouped under five broad headings: selling arms to China; engaging with Iran; destabilising Cuba; funding the Palestinian Authority; and co-operating with supra-national institutions, such as the UN, the Kyoto process and the International Criminal Court.

A common thread links these apparently unrelated disputes. In each of them, the US favours democracy over stability, the EU stability over democracy. Both unions are acting according to the DNA that was encoded at the time of their conception. The US was founded out of a popular rising against a distant and autocratic government, and so has a natural sympathy with freedom and self-government. The EU was founded following the horror of the Second World War, its patriarchs still haunted by the memory of the plebiscitary democracy that had preceded it. Perhaps understandably, the EU's founders believed that electoral majorities sometimes had to be tempered by the good sense and sobriety of professional administrators.

Historical experience has given European and American statesmen a very different *Weltanschauung* from that of their American counterparts. When an American politician looks at, for example, Israel, he sees a country like his own: a parliamentary democracy founded in adversity that elected its generals as its first leaders, and that maintained its commitment to representative government and the rule of law in difficult circumstances. Israel elicits his sympathy in the literal sense of fellow-feeling. The European, however, sees the displacement of a traditional and settled Arab society by a state based on the one ideology he disdains above all, that of national self-determination. Israel, after all, is the supreme embodiment of the national principle: the vindication, after 2,000 years, of a people's desire to form their own state. The EU, by contrast, is based on the notion that national loyalties are transient, arbitrary and ultimately discreditable. Simply by existing, Israel undermines the intellectual justification of European integration.

It is a similar story when it comes to Iran, or China or Cuba. The EU has never made a fetish out of democratic majorities, cheerfully disregarding referendums when they go the 'wrong' way. So, naturally enough, it applies the same standard beyond its borders, making allowances for autocratic regimes which seem at least to want to go in the right direction.

Ditto when it comes to supra-national bodies. Where Washington sees unelected technocrats seeking to overrule elected national governments, most Europeans see a framework of rules designed to bind irresponsible politicians, even if they happen to have secured a transient popular majority.

The interesting point, in the context of this book, is to observe how British foreign policy is drifting out of the gravitational pull of Washington and entering into orbit around Brussels. Although the United Kingdom is, in this as in so much else, mid-Atlantic, there is a discernible Europeanisation of our policy in all the instances cited. British ministers have visited Cuba and encouraged commercial links with the Communist regime there. Jack Straw was perhaps the most prominent of all EU politicians in seeking to cosy up to the ayatollahs in Tehran. Britain is an enthusiast, too, for the various international bodies that are so odious to Washington.

Much of this tendency has to do with the growing EU role in foreign policy, of which more later. But it also reflects the FCO's own guarded attitude to democracy. An exquisitely educated mandarin, who has learned over the years how to keep a series of unsophisticated ministers in check, might be excused for evincing a certain fellow feeling for an enlightened despot in another country, importuned on all sides to hold elections.

Transcending the nation-state

We saw earlier how the past 40 years have seen a sudden and unprecedented growth in international law. For hundreds of years, international law was strictly limited to the manner in which states dealt with each other. It covered maritime conventions, piracy, safe-conduct agreements, the treatment of ambassadors and, later, conventions on the prosecution of war. These days, as we discussed in the section on judicial activism, international law no longer stops at state frontiers. Treaties and conventions regulate everything from human rights to trade in endangered species, from the treatment of refugees to child labour. These accords are often treated by judges within the signatory states as part of their domestic jurisprudence. In other words, a country's adherence to an international legal code offers a way for its judiciary to by-pass its legislature.

To supporters of these international codes, this is precisely their attraction. They impose on nation-states an agenda that might never have been agreed by an elected legislature.

Once again, we come to the basic tension between those who believe in the supremacy of the ballot box – *vox populi, vox dei* – and those who would rather ensure that some spheres are left to the 'experts'. And those who are most prominent in this latter cause are, understandably, the 'experts' themselves. The international conventions by which they set such store were drawn up by them, or by people very like them. These accords ensure that what they see as humane and enlightened values are guaranteed against crowd-pleasing politicians – who may, in any case, have only an ephemeral mandate.

The problem is remediable. Every foreign treaty that imposes domestic obligations on Britain should be concluded only on a temporary basis. It should come before Parliament every year for re-adoption. If MPs believe that its provisions are being misinterpreted or wrongly applied, they will have the opportunity to demand its modification or, *in extremis*, its abrogation. This will prevent the constant accretion of international codes, each one with a standing bureaucracy dedicated to its constant expansion.

For international treaties are rarely limited to the paper on which they are signed. They also evolve secretariats, councils and commissions. Sometimes, these are limited in scope. The Commonwealth, for example, may issue advice to its members on domestic questions, but can impose no sanction other than exclusion from its ranks. The EU, on the other hand, has created a new legal order within the jurisdiction of its signatories, and given that legal order primacy over their domestic statutes.

In the eyes of the mandarin, such institutions formalise collaboration among states. They make impossible the smouldering grievances and secret diplomacy of the nineteenth century. Above all, they are a guarantee against that most dangerous of phenomena, nationalism.

The case for nationalism

What, though, do we mean by nationalism? The traditional definition is the desire of a people or language-group to form an independent and unitary state. Seen like that, is it so very different from what we mean by democracy?

To the democratic radicals of the eighteenth and nineteenth centuries, the two concepts were inseparable. To argue for government of, by and for the people instantly raised the question: what people? Within what unit should the electoral process be played out? The answer that the democrats came up with was, in truth, the only possible answer. Democracy works best within a territory whose inhabitants feel that they have enough in common one with another to accept government from each other's hands – in other words, within a nation.

Those who are keenest on supra-national institutions are, as a rule, also suspicious of the claims of secessionist movements within recognised states. The international community's immediate response to the Slovenian independence referendum in 1991, which triggered the conflict in Yugoslavia, was to inform all the constituent Yugoslav republics that they would not be recognised outside the federation. This policy eventually became untenable, but the same principle was applied when it came to insisting on the unity of a multi-ethnic Bosnia, and again when it came to holding Macedonia together. To this day, the UN and the EU refuse to countenance ethnographic frontiers in Kosovo or in Iraq.

There is a certain consistency in all this. Once again, the UN, the EU and the FCO value stability over democracy. For the truth is that supra-national states tend to work only to the extent that they deny democratic aspirations. The USSR and Yugoslavia worked as dictatorships, in the same way that the Habsburg and Ottoman empires had. The moment the subject peoples of these states were given the choice, they opted for self-government.

For Britain, the emphasis on preserving multi-national entities represents a complete reversal of what was once the basis of our foreign policy. Traditionally, Britain was a friend to national liberation movements. As Lord Randolph Churchill observed: 'England has always made the cause of nations her own cause. She supported the national movements of Germany and the Low Countries against Bonaparte. Her sympathy was with Greece, Hungary and Italy, and with the South American Republics.' Twice during the twentieth century, Britain would go on to embark on ruinous wars because a friendly country's sovereignty had been violated. Indeed, the notion that the Second World War was a battle on behalf of all nations would become a favourite refrain for Lord Randolph's son.

What has changed? Why do we now elevate the multi-ethnic state as an end in itself? Why do we now try to push other regions of the world into forming regional associations in mimicry of the EU? Much of the answer has to do with the contracting out of British strategic thinking to Brussels, a theme which we must now consider.

134

'Europe: your country'

It should by now be obvious to the reader why Britain's foreign-policy establishment is so determined on European integration. The EU is perhaps the supreme exemplar and beneficiary of the three characteristics identified as causes of the FCO's institutional failure: bureaucratic stasis, technocracy and dislike of nationalism.

First, European integration is, in the narrow sense, a conservative project, trapped in the assumptions of the 1950s, slow to adapt to change. To this day, supporters of deeper union talk about peace on the continent after years of war, the reconciliation of France and Germany and the entrenchment of democracy: all rather passé in the twenty-first century. At the same time, Euro-integrationists remain wedded to a social and economic model which seemed cutting-edge half a century ago, but which now appears ludicrously out of date.

Second, European integration is a technocratic and elitist project. We make this observation in no carping spirit: that is what it is meant to be. Jean Monnet, Robert Schuman and the other fathers of the European Communities had a profound distrust of untrammelled democracy which, in their eyes, had led to fascism and war. That is why they deliberately vested supreme power in an unelected European Commission – a body intended explicitly to be immune to public opinion. Complaining that the EU is undemocratic is like complaining that a cow is bovine, or a butterfly flighty: it is designed that way.

Third, European integration is based on the idea that nationalism is the worst of all political ideals. The EU's founding principle, repeated a hundred times a day even now, is that 'nationalism causes war'. This is, in fact, a highly questionable proposition: the worst wars of the modern era have been caused, not by nationalism, but by trans-national ideologies: Jacobinism, fascism, communism, Islamic fundamentalism. In each of these cases, national institutions and patriotic loyalties have tended to be a focus of resistance against tyranny. But no matter. To those who believe that voters are unduly excitable, and that the world is safer when run by a caste of international administrators, human rights lawyers and diplomats, the EU must seem a wonderful project.

Putting diplomats in charge

Small wonder then that, during the 1960s, the FCO began to agitate for British membership of the then European Economic Community. More than this, several motivated diplomats were determined to keep the application on course, regardless of the stated wishes of their elected ministers.

Their achievement is chronicled at length in *This Blessed Plot*, published in 1998 by the now deceased *Guardian* journalist Hugo Young. Young was perhaps the most solidly Europhile writer of his day, and his book rehearses most of the usual arguments for the EU, notably that Britain is forever losing out by being stand-offish and joining too late. He was also an exceptionally honest reporter, and was not too grand to roll up his sleeves and do some primary research. In particular, he tracked down many of the FCO officials who had mounted Britain's three applications for membership. Now retired (usually to the South of France) these men spoke frankly about how they had, on occasion, acted directly contrary to the stated wishes of the government in order to pursue what they regarded as the national interest. Young, of course, regards their attitude with approval, but the general reader is left gasping. This is how he summarised what took place during the 1960s:

An elite regiment was taking shape [in the FCO]. Europe wasn't yet the path of choice for every ambitious diplomat, but it promised to be much more interesting than the Commonwealth, and offered a prospect of influence greater than anything else available to a second-order power. By 1963, a corps of diplomats was present in and around the Foreign Office who saw the future for both themselves and their country inside Europe. The interests of their country and their careers coincided. It was an appealing symbiosis.

Of course diplomats approve of the EU: it was built by and for people like them. The Norwegian and Swiss diplomatic corps are as desperate to join now as the FCO was 40 years ago. What is staggering about Young's meticulously researched book is the insouciance with which these men – for reasons which, as he admits, were as much personal as ideological – were able to pursue their agenda independently of what the country had decided at the ballot box.

The EU is not just a consequence of the tendencies we identified in the previous chapter; it also encourages them within its constituent states. It does so partly by removing decision-making one tier further from the public, and thus providing a sense of insulation to national politicians. But it does so more immediately by directing the foreign policies of its members.

A European foreign policy

Many British politicians in both parties continue to talk quaintly about the need to resist a common European foreign policy. In fact, such a foreign policy is already operative. Go to any non-European capital and you will find that the EU mission dwarfs the national embassies. And why not? What used to be the chief business of national embassies has already been ceded to Brussels. One hundred per cent of trade policy and ninety-nine per cent of development aid is controlled by the EU, leaving the national missions with little to do beyond promoting tourism and hosting visiting ministers from their home states.

Go back to the five areas which we identified as the main causes of friction between Brussels and Washington: the Chinese arms embargo, the Iranian nuclear programme, the future of Cuba, the treatment of Hamas and the status of supra-national institutions. In all these areas, a common European foreign policy applies. Member states may theoretically have the right to pursue different approaches in these areas; in practice, it would never occur to their foreign services to do so.

And what is the most important aim of European foreign policy? To foster integration on the EU model in other continents. It is little appreciated how much the various regional associations – the Central American Union, ASEAN, the African Union and the rest – owe to the EU. From the first, the EU has financed and promoted regional integration campaigns. It sometimes even makes its trade and aid deals conditional on a state's participation in such associations. And this, by default, also becomes the chief goal of the 27 member states. Ask, say, the British Ambassador to Montevideo to define the UK's key strategic goal in Uruguay, and he will talk about turning Mercosur into a proper political union. Our national interests are redefined to reflect, not just the ambitions of the European

Commission, but the prejudices of our diplomatic corps. As Hugo Young might say, it is an appealing symbiosis.

The EU has allowed many Whitehall departments, not just the FCO, to make policy with minimal political interference. It is time to consider how to restore that political interference which, in the last analysis, distinguishes a democracy from a dictatorship.

Restoring parliamentary supremacy

Our parliament is unusually weak in the field of foreign affairs. Through a quirk of history, as we saw earlier in a domestic context, the Prime Minister has inherited more or less intact the executive powers that once attached to the monarchy. Diplomatic appointments, the contracting of treaties and national defence are all controlled by Downing Street under Crown Prerogative powers.

The peculiar feebleness of our legislature, even relative to other EU states, is illustrated whenever a European treaty needs to be implemented. Whereas most of the other members have constitutions that require parliamentary ratification or, in some cases, referendums, British MPs find that large chunks of the treaties can be approved without passing through the House of Commons. The signature of the Foreign Secretary, acting on behalf of the Sovereign, is all that is required.

For a long time, this state of affairs was regarded as indefensible in theory, but acceptable in practice. Perhaps because of their doubts about its fairness, successive prime ministers tended to exercise their Crown Prerogative powers with discretion. Criticism of the dispensation was more or less limited to Tony Benn. This acceptance began to wane when the same powers were used to ram through the Maastricht Treaty, but there was still little clamour for constitutional change.

Then, in June 2005, in *Direct Democracy*, we proposed that the appointment powers exercised under Crown Prerogative be transferred to Parliament. Three months later, to Tony Benn's surprise and delight, David Cameron committed a future Conservative government to the policy.

Applied to the field of foreign affairs, this would have two main consequences. First, it would give the House of Commons treaty-making powers, similar to those enjoyed by the US Senate and by several other parliamentary chambers around the world. On the principle that no parliament may bind its successor, such treaties would no longer be contracted indefinitely. Rather, they would be placed regularly before the Chamber – ideally on an annual basis – for re-adoption. If they were not specifically endorsed, they would be deemed to lapse.

The idea of time-limited Acts – 'sunset clauses'– is not a new one. The Prevention of Terrorism Act was voted on every year throughout most of the 1970s and 1980s. Nor should the principle be limited to foreign policy. A more widespread use of the sunset clauses would constrain the otherwise ever-growing corpus of legislation. But the application of the doctrine to the field of international relations would have one especially happy consequence: it would remind the agencies and secretariats established by international accords that they had a limited mandate and that expanding their powers beyond those envisaged by the signatory states might lead to those states withdrawing.

It would also act as a check on one of the more curious of political phenomena, namely the way in which national ministers crave the approval of their foreign counterparts. Almost all national parliaments complain that their ministers 'go native' when negotiating international deals, and exceed the mandate bestowed on them by their MPs. This would plainly be less likely to occur if ministers knew that whatever they agreed would have to be approved by Parliament, not just once, but in perpetuity.

The second major consequence of the abolition of Crown Prerogative would be an end to the appointment and promotion of diplomats without political scrutiny. The situation described by Hugo Young in *This Blessed Plot* would simply not arise; or, if it did, it could be instantly remedied.

When George Shultz was US Secretary of State in the 1980s, he had a routine for appointing American ambassadors. He would ask them to point to their country on a large map in his office. They would duly point to Guinea Bissau (or wherever). 'Nope,' he would tell them, tapping the USA, '*this* is your country.'

It is perhaps no coincidence that the US, which has always had a degree of legislative control over both appointments and treaties, has such a clearly defined strategic vision and such a readiness to deploy proportionate force in defence of its interests. Nor can it be entirely coincidental that, when Parliament was supreme, and our diplomatic service small and subordinate, we too were willing to project our interests.

Some of the greatest of our foreign policy initiatives were undertaken as a direct result of popular pressure, expressed through parliamentary representation. The extirpation of the slave trade was led by public opinion. The support for liberal regimes abroad, too, was populist in origin. Foreign policy could, indeed, become the major electoral question of the day, as during Gladstone's Midlothian campaign.

The democratisation of diplomacy ought to be especially attractive for Conservatives. In the rest of the world, and especially in other Anglosphere countries, parties of the Centre-Right derive a substantial measure of their electoral appeal from being the more trusted on foreign affairs. In Britain, by contrast, politicians have contracted out large chunks of international relations to the permanent functionaries in Whitehall and, especially, Brussels. In consequence, the issue has slipped from the electoral agenda.

A British foreign policy

It is beyond the scope of this book to define precisely how a comprehensive and consistent British foreign policy would operate. In general, we should rediscover our sympathy for national movements. We should prefer countries to be united by trade than by political structures. We should sponsor the spread of individual liberty and property rights, and thereby guarantee our own prosperity as a commercial nation. We should work with friends and allies around the world instead of narrowing our horizons to Europe. We should put our faith in elected national politicians rather than remote supranational bureaucracies. We should combine military preparedness with a preference for non-intervention: war is a terrible destroyer of freedom as well as of people and property. An ability to intervene, combined with a reluctance to become entangled – splendid isolation as the policy came to be known in retrospect – brought Britain to its highest point as a nation.

None of these things is possible, however, until foreign policy is wrenched back out of the grasp of EU officials and their British auxiliaries. We must make the question of how Britain relates to other nations a question for the British people, either through their elected representatives or, directly, through referendums.

The Europe of Nations Myth

Britain needs a wholly different relationship with the EU. We are not going to waste words on what kind of Europe we might ideally have wanted; rather, we shall address ourselves to the practical question of how Britain ought to relate to the Europe that has in fact taken shape on its doorstep.

Asking, 'What kind of Europe do we want?' is both presumptuous and dishonest. Presumptuous because it is not in Britain's gift to dictate how the other states of the EU should relate one to another; and dishonest because, in holding out the prospect of a different Europe from the one in fact on offer, it perpetrates a falsehood.

This falsehood has persisted for as long as EU membership has been an issue in British politics. We may call it, as a form of shorthand, the Europe of Nations Myth. It runs roughly as follows. The EU is not a settled system but an evolving experiment. Each of its members has its own national perspectives. By getting stuck in wholeheartedly, making some concessions to prove its good faith, and then arguing from the inside, Britain can arrest the tendencies it dislikes. Having demonstrated its *communautaire* credentials, it will be in a much better position to turn the EU away from protectionism, centralisation and political integration, and towards a looser form of association.

The Europe of Nations Myth formed the basis of Britain's original application to the EEC under Harold Macmillan. The deliberations of the Cabinet's European Association Committee were summarised in a report by the Cabinet Secretary, Sir Norman Brook, on 6 July 1960, which concluded thus:

The effects of any eventual loss of sovereignty would be mitigated:

1. by our participation in majority voting in the Council of Ministes and by our being able to influence the Commission's work;

> *2. if resistance to Federalism on the part of some of the other Governments continues which our membership might be expected to encourage.*

Even in Macmillan's day, this was wishful thinking, as the most cursory reading of contemporary EEC communiqués would have shown. Nonetheless, with the EEC only three years old, the error was perhaps excusable. It is harder to forgive today, when we have half a century of empirical evidence to the effect that the European Treaties mean what they say about 'ever-closer union'. Yet each British Prime Minister comes to office believing that, by being positive and constructive, he will somehow be able to talk the other members out of their long-held and long-stated objective of amalgamation.

Sooner or later, this optimism turns sour. It happened to Margaret Thatcher in 1988. Having begun her term as Tory leader by campaigning for EEC membership in a hideous jumper made up of the flags of the then nine member states, she ended it with her famous reaction to Jacques Delors' plans for closer integration: 'No. No. No.' It happened to John Major in 1996. In his first important speech as Prime Minister in 1990, Major had promised an audience in Bonn that he would 'put Britain where it has always belonged: at the very heart of Europe'; yet he finished his premiership by ordering his ministers to obstruct all EU business in protest at the beef ban. It happened to Tony Blair in 2005. At his first party conference as Labour leader in 1994, Blair told delegates: 'Under my leadership, Britain will never be isolated or left behind in Europe.' Eleven years later, he likened Brussels to Jericho, telling startled MEPs that the people were blowing their horns outside the city walls.

Each of these leaders learned the hard way that diplomacy works on the basis of present interests, not past gratitude. As far as the other member states are concerned, Britain signed up to the objective of political union – the *finalité politique* as it is known in Euro-jargon – when it joined. Agreeing to closer integration is, in their eyes, the basic condition of membership, clearly stated in the founding treaties, rather than a special concession meriting additional reward. To expect the Continental states to tear up their past treaties simply to favour British domestic opinion is breathtakingly arrogant.

Yet still the Europe of Nations Myth persists. Ask almost any British politician what he thinks about Europe and he will say something like: 'I believe in a Europe of independent states, trading with each other, working together for the common good, and remaining open to the rest of the world.' Most people in Britain would happily sign up to such a Europe. The trouble is that this is not where the EU is going. Even as things stand today – without factoring in the coming integration in the fields of justice and home affairs, diplomatic representation, human rights, immigration and defence proposed in the Lisbon Treaty – we are further than we have ever been from such a dispensation. When politicians pretend, despite all the evidence, that the process can somehow be reversed, they are not engaging in a harmless daydream: they are perpetrating a deceit on their electorate.

The honest question is not 'Do we want a politically integrated EU or a Europe of Nations?' Rather, it is: 'Given that the EU is set on political integration, what kind of relationship ought Britain to have with it?'

The interesting thing about the Europe of Nations Myth is that its strain mutates in each generation. There is always an apparently plausible reason for thinking that the EU is about to take a wholly new direction. Sometimes it is claimed that a rising politician somewhere on the Continent will alter the geometry of the EU. Absurd as it now sounds, Jacques Chirac, José-María Aznar, Silvio Berlusconi and even Gerhard Schröder were all written up prior to their elections as potential British allies on European issues. So, more recently, was Nicolas Sarkozy.

There are two contemporary variants of the Europe of Nations Myth: 'Ah, but the new member countries are much closer to Britain in their thinking'; and 'Surely these 'no' votes have changed everything.'

We have, of course, heard it all before. Every enlargement round is hailed in Britain as spelling the end of the federalist enterprise. It will no longer be possible, runs the reasoning, to apply uniform policies to an EU with such varied conditions and needs. Yet, in practice, each successive expansion has been linked to a new federalising treaty. The entry of Spain and Portugal in 1986 was followed by the Single European Act. The admission of Austria, Sweden and Finland in 1995 led promptly to the Amsterdam and Nice

Treaties. The assimilation of the ten ex-Communists states, plus Malta and Cyprus, was accompanied by the European Constitution, the most ambitious power-grab in the history of the Union.

The argument that the ex-Communist countries will alter the orientation of the EU because of their relatively *souverainiste* outlook would surely have applied even more strongly to Britain's own accession in 1973. But the peoples of Poland, Estonia and the rest will soon discover, as the British have done, that their views have little impact on their representatives in Brussels.

Ignoring the 'no' votes

Similarly, the idea that the recent 'no' votes in France, the Netherlands and Ireland will force EU leaders back to the drawing board is not borne out by history. The same argument was made when Denmark voted against Maastricht, when Ireland voted against Nice – and, for that matter, when the markets voted against the Exchange Rate Mechanism. In each case, the EU simply carried on as though nothing had changed. It is doing the same today. Large parts of the constitution are being implemented as though the 'no' votes had not happened. EU judges are treating the Charter of Fundamental Rights as justiciable, even though it has no binding force outside the constitution. The integration of criminal justice, including the creation of an EU prosecution service, is continuing apace. The EU has established dozens of institutions and policies that have no legal basis without the constitution: the European Defence Agency, the External Borders Agency, the Human Rights Institute, politico-military structures, a collective security clause, a space policy, a diplomatic service.

How much more does Brussels have to do to shake us out of our complacency? In its refusal to accept the verdict of the French, Dutch and Irish electorates, the EU has demonstrated beyond doubt that no force, internal or external, will check the advance towards political union – neither popular opposition not its own rule-book. The time has come to snap out of our delusion, look honestly at where the EU is going, and decide how Britain ought to relate to it.

What kind of Britain do we want?

Rather than asking 'What kind of Europe do we want', we should ponder a more pertinent question – one, at any rate, that is within our gift to affect – namely 'What kind of *Britain* do we want?'

To start at the most basic level, everyone agrees that Britain should be democratic and free. But these are not just hooray-words; they have specific meanings, and there are degrees of democracy and freedom. When decisions are taken by unelected functionaries rather than by elected representatives, a state is less democratic, for all that it may hold regular elections. When citizens are bossed about by the government, a state is less free, for all that it may respect basic human rights.

As J S Mill wrote:

If the roads, the railways, the banks, the insurance offices, the great joint stock companies, the universities, and the public charities, were all of them branches of the government; if, in addition, the municipal corporations and local boards, with all that now devolves on them, became departments of the central administration; if the employees of all these different enterprises were appointed and paid by the government, and looked to the government for every rise in life; not all the freedom of the press and popular constitution of the legislature would make this country free otherwise than in name.

By these criteria, there are several ways in which the United Kingdom could be made more democratic and more free. Many of the powers currently exercised by central government could be devolved, either directly to the citizen or to a lower level of administration. Many of the officials whose decisions affect our lives could be made directly accountable at the ballot box.

It is worth repeating the three principles that have informed our approach throughout this book:

- That decisions should be taken as closely as possible to the people they affect

- That decision-makers should be directly accountable
- That citizens should be free from state coercion

To this end, we have set out a number of proposals: self-financing local councils, elected Sheriffs, pluralism in healthcare, legislative referendums, choice in education and much more. The reader may by now have noticed that many of these ideas are incompatible with EU membership. This is true on two levels. First, some of our specific proposals are at odds with EU law: replacing VAT with a Local Sales Tax, allowing Parliament to set an annual quota for the number of people allowed to settle in Britain, passing a Reserve Powers Act to guarantee the supremacy of the legislature against judicial activism.

More seriously, though, the entire philosophy which underpins our ideas – that of devolution to the lowest possible level – is impossible to reconcile with European integration. If we want decisions to be taken as closely as possible to the people they affect, they plainly should not be taken in Brussels. If we prefer elected bodies to quangos, we can hardly submit ourselves to the biggest quango of all, namely the European Commission. If we believe in individual liberty, we naturally rebel against the idea of a distant bureaucracy churning out restrictive regulations. Above all, if we want MPs to be able to keep their promises, they must be in a position to implement the manifestos on which they were elected.

Politicians do not have this power in contemporary Britain. The EU, as such, may not dominate domestic election campaigns, but it makes its malign, brooding presence felt nonetheless. There it sits like Banquo's ghost, unseen by most voters, but shaking its gory locks at the party leaders, who know that they must draw up their manifestos within the parameters allowed by EU law. There was a dramatic illustration of this in March 2005, when Michael Howard announced that a future Conservative Government would set an upper limit to the number of immigrants entering Britain and a separate quota for refugees, only to be told that this would contravene EU law. The same phenomenon is at work across much of government policy. No party can promise to rescue Britain's countryside as long as we are in the Common Agricultural Policy.

No party can offer to treat our fishing grounds as the renewable resource they ought to be while we are bound by the Common Fisheries Policy. No party can recognise the principles of free contract and deregulation while we are subject to the Social Chapter.

Our objective is to have a Britain in which we favour the citizen over the state, the elected representative over the quango, and the local councillor over Whitehall. Such a Britain is incompatible, in theory and in practice, with the EU.

It is no coincidence that the European state which comes closest to the practice of direct democracy, Switzerland, has voted repeatedly against a closer association with Brussels. Switzerland operates a highly diffused system in which individual cantons are in some ways more sovereign than member states of the EU. The two main reasons given by Swiss voters for opposing EU membership are that they want to keep the fiscal autonomy of the cantons, including their right to set their own rates of VAT, and that they believe that their tradition of local legislative referendums would run up against EU law. They are right.

What is the alternative?

A mistake made by both sides in the European debate is to present the issue as an all-or-nothing choice between integration and isolation – or, depending on your point of view, between subjugation and independence. In reality, as we look around Europe, we see that there are many degrees of association with the EU that fall short of full membership.

The three non-EU members of the European Economic Area, Norway, Iceland and Liechtenstein, maintain their membership of the single market through common EEA institutions – a court, a commission and so on. Switzerland, like these three countries, is a member of the European Free Trade Area, EFTA, but is outside the EEA, relying instead on a series of sectoral treaties negotiated with the EU in the early 1990s. The Channel Islands are inside the single market, but outside the EU, and therefore exempt from the Common Agricultural Policy, the Common Fisheries Policy and many financial regulations. Turkey is a member of the customs union, but not of the common political institutions. Greenland, which left the EU following a referendum in 1984, nonetheless maintains large chunk of its old rights and obligations under the common market.

Equally, within the EU itself, there are different levels of integration. Some countries are in the Euro, others outside it. Some have specific opt-outs from elements of the Treaties. The UK and Ireland are outside the Schengen zone – the EU's border-free area – while several non-EU states, including Norway, Iceland and, following a referendum in 2005, Switzerland, are inside it.

The more we consider the broad picture, the harder it is to sustain the idea that EU membership is a whole hog, *totus porcus*, option. It would be more accurate to think of integration on an issue-by-issue basis: defence, fisheries, free movement of people and so on. It is plainly feasible to participate in some of these areas but not others.

Let us go back to first principles and ask what interests Britain would wish to secure in its relations with the rest of the EU. The following list is not comprehensive, but it may serve us as a useful place to start. The United Kingdom should aim:

- To preserve its access to European markets
- To enjoy free-trade arrangements with non-EU states
- To attract inward investment from EU and non-EU sources by managing a competitive and deregulated economy
- To maintain its military and diplomatic alliances with Europe, the Commonwealth and the United States
- To minimise its budgetary contributions to Brussels
- To control its territorial resources, including energy and fisheries
- To suit agricultural policy to the needs of its own farmers
- To co-operate with its neighbours on cross-border issues, such as environmental pollution
- To work with the rest of Europe in the fight against international crime and terrorism
- To restore the supremacy of Parliament

Is it possible to secure most, or even all, of these goals? Would the other member states be content to let Britain participate only in those common policies that suited it? While it is obviously impossible to answer these questions definitively, we can learn from the way in which some non-EU states maintain their position within Europe's markets and their voice in Europe's counsels. The four EFTA countries, in particular, come close to meeting these objectives, *mutatis mutandis*. In reality, there is every reason to assume that Britain could secure an even more attractive settlement than the EFTA states, both because it is an existing member of the EU, and because it has a far larger economy – one, incidentally, that has run a huge trade deficit with the other member states over the 30 years of its membership. So Britain should look on EFTA as, so to speak, the baseline: minimum terms, on which it would aim to improve.

How EFTA works

Even within EFTA there are considerable variations between what each country has negotiated. Iceland has opted out of elements of free transport in order to secure its unique fauna. Norway, by contrast, has been keen to join several aspects of EU policy which go beyond the EEA accord, notably on foreign policy and international aid. Switzerland is outside the EEA, instead relying on bilateral treaties. Nonetheless, some things can be said of all four countries.

They are all covered by the Four Freedoms of the Single Market – free movement, that is, of goods, services, people and capital. Their businesses and citizens face no discrimination of any kind *vis-à-vis* those of the EU. Yet these countries are outside the Common Agricultural and Fisheries Policies, in charge of their own immigration policies, free to settle human rights questions themselves and able to negotiate free-trade accords with non-EU states. They remain sovereign democracies, and make only token contributions to the EU budget.

Unsurprisingly, this settlement has made them far more prosperous than the states of the EU: GDP per capita in EFTA is 214 per cent of that in the EU. Able to participate in the free market, but exempt from many of the EU's social and employment rules, EFTA states get the best of all worlds.

It is true that businesses in EFTA states must meet EU standards when selling to the EU – as exporters the world over must do. But they are not forced to apply these standards to their domestic commercial activity – at least, not on anything like the scale of their EU counterparts. It is interesting to note that every one of the EFTA countries exports more per head to the EU than does Britain. EFTA is a living, thriving refutation of the argument that Britain is too small to flourish on its own, and must be part of a larger European polity.

It is sometimes argued that the EFTA countries are at a disadvantage because they are forced to implement EU laws over whose drafting they have had little say. This is true, but it is a problem in theory rather than in practice. Remember that the legislation in question covers only a small and clearly delineated part of the EFTA countries' public life. Huge areas of policy are wholly excluded: agriculture, fisheries, aspects of social policy and employment law, foreign affairs, defence, criminal justice, most of immigration and asylum policy and the Charter of Fundamental Rights. Almost all these directives are technical in nature, dealing principally with the adoption of common standards for the facilitation of trade. Since the EEA Treaty was signed in 1992, the implementation of 3,000 EU legal acts has required only 49 changes of the law in Norway and Iceland (Liechtenstein joined later). And Switzerland is completely exempt from such legislation, adopting parallel laws only when it believes that they are advantageous.

British Euro-enthusiasts like to claim that the EFTA countries are each, in different ways, unique. 'You can't compare us to Iceland,' they say, 'Iceland has fish.' So, of course, would Britain if it were not subject to the Common Fisheries Policy. 'We're nothing like Norway,' they continue. 'Norway has oil.' Indeed. And Britain is the EU's only net exporter of oil, which is why it should be so concerned about the repeated attempts to make energy supplies a common European resource. 'Switzerland is a special case,' they protest. 'They have financial services.' And Britain, in the City of London, has the EU's – arguably the world's – leading financial centre, although it is unlikely to remain so if Brussels continues to harmonise taxes and impose regulations on takeovers, investment advice and banking practices.

Then, in a delicious back-flip, pro-Europeans try a new argument. 'But we're nothing like these EFTA countries,' they say. 'They're much *smaller* than us.' This is a refreshing change from their usual contention, *viz.* that Britain is too small to prosper outside the EU. What they probably mean by it, to be fair, is that Britain is a country with global interests. The tiddlers may be able to absent themselves from the councils of Europe, runs the reasoning, but it would be harder for us to do so. Yet not even this argument stands up.

For an example of a country with truly impressive global reach, consider Norway. Norwegian diplomats are playing a key role in the Middle East, Sudan, South East Asia and Sri Lanka. Being outside the EU's cumbersome development programmes, they are able to use their overseas aid as an instrument of foreign policy. They are regarded as reliable, neutral arbitrators of third country disputes. How much of this would still be true if they were one of the EU's smaller members? As a former Norwegian ambassador to London put it:

Our worst time was just before the 1994 referendum [on EU membership]. Since everyone assumed that we were going to join, I was always being asked to meetings with my 15 European counterparts. Often, I wouldn't even get to speak. Once we voted 'no', people had to start dealing with me separately again.

The Swiss, although deeply suspicious of international entanglements, nonetheless manage to host most of the big international organisations, including the Red Cross, large chunks of the UN, FIFA and the International Olympics Committee. Iceland, with a population about the size of Croydon's, has received state visits from four US Presidents, two Russian leaders and, most recently, the Chinese premier, who stayed for several days to study the island's economic success.

The EFTA countries have evidently judged that they have more influence by operating foreign policies of their own than they would have as tiny statelets within the EU. Surely Britain, with immense global experience, the fifth largest economy in the world and the fourth military power, would be able to retain an international presence without having to go through Brussels.

We are not arguing for an exact replication of what the EFTA countries have negotiated. Britain is in a different and, indeed, relatively advantageous position. Our point rather, is that if these tiny countries, relying on traditional diplomacy and bilateral accords, have managed to secure themselves advantageous deals, surely Britain, with its population of 60 million, a maritime nation whose colonising and enterprising energies have touched every continent, would be able to negotiate terms at least as favourable.

In doing so, Britain would also be assisting the more integrationist states, removing its constant carping and vetoing from their deliberations. By allowing the core, Carolingian countries to pursue their objective of full amalgamation, while it – and perhaps some of the other peripheral nations – stood aside as a friend and sponsor, Britain would restore harmony to the concert of Europe. The federalist countries would lose a bad tenant, and gain a good neighbour.

Britain, for its part, would be freer, more democratic and wealthier. Abroad, it would be able to pursue a foreign policy in accordance with its own traditions and interests. At home, it could at last begin to unbundle powers from Whitehall. But parliamentary supremacy is a necessary first step. At present, an astonishing 84 per cent of national legislation in EU member states derives from Brussels. Before those powers can be devolved to local councils and private citizens, they must first be repatriated from the EU.

10. Direct democracy

➢ The right of popular legislative initiative
➢ The right to initiate a referendum to block contentious new laws
➢ Referendums on any proposed constitutional changes
➢ Local referendums

Every British schoolchild is taught – or at any rate used to be taught – that this country is unique in not having a written constitution. The great constitutionalists of the past – Bagehot, Dicey, Erskine May – believed that the British system succeeded precisely because it was based on practice rather than theory, on the accreted wisdom of the ages rather than the arrogance of a single generation seeking to impose its settlement in perpetuity. All sorts of habits and conventions that would never have been adopted from first principles nonetheless turned out to work rather well, and so were sanctified by usage.

True, there was no single document guaranteeing the rights of the citizen or limiting the powers of the state (though such rights and limitations could be found in a number of acts stretching back to Magna Carta). Instead, there was parliamentary supremacy. Rather than contracting out responsibility for the defence of their liberties to a constitutional court, the British took immediate responsibility for them through the ballot box. And – so traditional constitutional theory held – the system worked very well. To the envy of other countries, it had guaranteed stability, without descent into either revolution or dictatorship.

There was much in this theory. But the constitutional settlement described by the old authorities has been displaced. No longer does Britain have a sovereign Parliament in place of a written constitution. Parliament has surrendered its prerogatives to the quango state at home and to the EU abroad. The Whipping system means that, in any event, Parliament is no longer any kind of check on the executive. In short, the UK now has a system where the government is unconstrained: neither the legislature nor a written constitution can arrest its powers.

In recent years, we have seen constitutional changes of enormous importance enacted more or less on the say-so of the Prime Minister, changes which no other head of government in the democratic world could order: the abolition of the office of Lord Chancellor; the disfranchisement of a majority of members of the Upper House; the creation of a supreme court. If Angela Merkel had wanted to abolish the Bundesrat, or George Bush to allow presidents to serve for a third term, they would have needed to initiate a major process of constitutional amendment. No such check applies to the British Prime Minister: all he needs is a vote in a Parliament controlled by his Whips.

The old model – the model that we were brought up to be proud of – no longer applies. We have neither the protection of constitutional rights nor that of democratic accountability. Without noticing it, we have opened the door to a subtle and polite despotism.

In this book, we have set out a number of ways to tilt the balance back from the executive branch of government to the legislative. We have also recommended the one reform that would make Parliament independent of the government in practice as well as in theory: open primaries. But these changes alone will not guarantee full democracy. The sovereignty of Parliament, after all, was only ever defensible as a guarantee of the sovereignty of the people. If there are more direct ways of guaranteeing that sovereignty, we should embrace them.

Parliamentary or plebiscitary democracy?

Referendums have traditionally been viewed with some distaste in Britain, for precisely the reasons just outlined. Convinced of the superiority of our system of parliamentary rule, we viewed the referendum as a toy for excitable Continentals: 'a device for demagogues and dictators,' as Clement Attlee put it.

This attitude has shifted in recent years, for three reasons. First, it is becoming painfully obvious that parliamentary supremacy no longer exists, and MPs have fallen commensurately in public esteem. Second, the repeated denials of referendums on successive European treaties, often in violation of previous promises, have convinced many people that, far from diminishing representative democracy, referendums would buttress it. And third, the sheer number of referendums in recent years – there have been 47 in total,

45 of them since 1997 – has made it impossible to claim that plebiscites are incompatible with the British constitution.

We are convinced that referendums strengthen parliamentary sovereignty. Look at the countries which favour them. The US, which makes regular use of referendums in many of its states, is nonetheless so jealous of its sovereignty that it remains outside many international associations, from the Kyoto process to the International Criminal Court. Switzerland, the most referendum-prone state in the world, is touchier still, having only very recently agreed to join the United Nations.

That said, Britain has its own traditions and its own values. We should not import another country's system *tout entier*, but rather adapt the referendum to our own institutions. In particular, given the traditional centrality of Parliament in our national life, we are reluctant to create an extra-parliamentary mechanism for the generation of new legislation. That caveat, however, does not apply to the use of referendums to *block* proposed changes.

We propose four mechanisms of direct democracy, all of them compatible with our constitutional practice: the right of popular initiative; the veto referendum; the constitutional referendum; and the local referendum.

The right of popular initiative
Several states allow legislation to be proposed directly by the public, bypassing the legislature. If a certain number of signatures is gathered, a proposition is automatically put to a referendum and, if carried, it gains binding force. The 'Citizens' Initiative' exists, in one form or another, in around half the US states, as well as Switzerland, Austria, Italy, New Zealand, Hungary, Lithuania and Slovakia. In many of these countries, the threshold for the number of signatures required is so high that the right is more theoretical than real. But popular initiative does play a role in parts of the US and, especially, Switzerland, where issues as diverse as taxation, immigration and environmental protection are regularly put to popular vote.

The system has clear attractions. It shifts power from politicians to people. It educates and informs the electorate. Voters who have to take their own decisions are less likely to moan that 'they should do something'. It prevents the political class from pursuing an agenda at odds with that of the rest of the country – which is to say, it prevents the formation of a political class in the first place.

The Swiss system of direct democracy has enemies. Many Swiss MPs privately detest it, though few say so openly. Pressure groups and non-governmental organisations are even more opposed: referendums make it much harder for a single lobby to capture government policy. But the referendum has a powerful defence: itself. Unable to abolish the system without a referendum, Swiss politicians, civil servants and voluntary sector activists are obliged to work within the constraints of public opinion.

For all these advantages, though, it is hard to see how Swiss-style direct democracy could simply be grafted on to British institutions. The potency of popular initiative in Switzerland is matched by a weakness in its representative institutions. The federal parliament is, in effect, a part-time assembly. The federal cabinet is a permanent coalition in which all the parties are represented according to a formula worked out in the 1920s.

We have already discussed the advantages of reducing the number of MPs and cutting the number of days when Parliament is in session. The idea of 'citizen legislators' – MPs who would meet rarely, draw only token salaries to compensate them for their time, and be expected to carry on with whatever job they previously had – is hardly a foreign import. It was how Britain administered itself during its rise to greatness.

Nonetheless, our Parliament has a history, a dignity and a legitimacy unmatched in the world. As Enoch Powell put it: 'Parliament is a word of magic and power in this country.' Our aim should be to import the key advantage of the Citizens' Initiative – that it prevents politicians from ignoring matters of overwhelming public concern – without derogating from parliamentary sovereignty. The way to do this is through People's Bills: legislative proposals put on the agenda of the House of Commons having attracted popular support in petitions. There would be no obligation on MPs to pass the Bills; but they would have to debate and vote on them, and then be held to account for how they voted.

People's Bills would be tabled as follows.

1. Any British citizen on the electoral register might submit a written proposal to the House of Commons Table Office, along with an administration fee and a deposit.

2. The Table Office Clerk would determine the wording of the proposed petition and the subsequent Bill, perhaps, as in New Zealand, having invited a wider public consultation. The Clerk would determine that no similar petition had been submitted within the previous five years. The Clerk would also be empowered, with the approval of the Speaker, to disallow frivolous proposals. The withdrawal of the proposal, or the death of the petitioner, would cause the proposal to lapse automatically.

3. The organisers would then have until the end of that parliamentary session to gather signatures for their proposal. Signatures could be collected online as well as conventionally, with petitioners providing names and addresses. The sole stipulation would be that every petitioner be a registered voter and a British national.

4. Instead of setting a threshold for the requisite number of signatures, as happens abroad, we suggest that the six proposals with the most support be tabled. The other proposals would fall at this stage, and the petitioners would lose their deposits.

5. The six most popular proposals would then be presented to the new Parliament. Having read out her Government's Bills, the Queen would end her Speech by proposing her People's Bills. These would be voted on in order of popularity, with a full day in government time being set aside for each one. MPs would be free to amend the Bills as well, obviously, as to vote against them.

Most of the opposition to Citizens' Initiatives takes one of three forms. It is alleged that the laws produced by the system are shoddy and ill-considered; that they are expensive and time-consuming; and that they are illiberal and populist.

None of these concerns is validated by the empirical evidence. As Mads Qvortup showed in *Supply Side Politics* (Centre for Policy Studies, 2005), the evidence from abroad is that citizens' bills tend to be better drafted, and in need of less amendment, than those proposed by governments. Nor would the drafting of the legislation be any more expensive than that of any other Bill; and the cost of organising the petitions would be borne by the sponsors of the proposal, not the taxpayer.

As for populism – the usual one-line put-down by opponents of direct democracy is 'would you want a referendum on bringing back hanging?' – again, this is not sustained by the evidence. The death penalty has been abolished by referendum more frequently than supported, most recently in Ireland in 2001. True, there are some states in the US where capital punishment has been introduced by referendum. Yet there are more states where it has been introduced by state legislatures. Frederick Boehmke has shown that the initiative-operating states are less likely to adopt the death penalty than other states.

The US is, in fact, a useful case study. With 24 states operating Citizens' Initiatives in one form or another, and 26 not, we can make like-with-like comparisons. The results are telling. Far from reducing participation in legislative elections, popular initiative seems to increase it: as David Schmidt shows in *Citizen Lawmakers*, turnout is five per cent higher in states where there are referendums than in states where there are not. Legislation in those states is lighter and better drafted. And, most surprisingly of all, GDP is higher.

In short, the evidence is that popular ballots make people better citizens. As Keith Joseph put it in a different context: 'Give people responsibility and you will make them responsible.'

But, even if we are wrong, our proposal retains an ultimate veto by Parliament. MPs would not be in a position of having legislation forced on them. They would, however, have to take sides on issues of concern to their constituents, and explain their reasoning.

The right to a blocking referendum
Except in Switzerland and the Western states of the US, the right to

popular initiative is used only rarely. Sometimes, this is because the threshold for signatures is dauntingly high: in New Zealand, for instance, it is ten per cent. In Lithuania, where it has effected significant changes in policy, it has nonetheless been activated only three times since its inception in the 1990s.

Of far more importance to Swiss supporters of direct democracy is the veto referendum: the ability to require a referendum before a contentious piece of legislation comes into force.

Again, many Swiss MPs loathe the system, complaining that it skews their polity towards conservatism. The Swiss electorate is often sceptical of its politicians' pet projects. Referendums have rejected major changes in policy that appealed to the political class: higher federal taxes, more generous immigration rules, a closer association with the EU. In these and other cases, however, the very fact of holding the referendum resulted in a far better and more informed debate than in most countries. The hostility to EU membership, for example, does not reflect xenophobia: the Swiss are among the most cosmopolitan and multi-lingual of all Europeans. The main arguments of the 'No' campaign were that EU membership would weaken cantonal autonomy, harmonise taxation, diminish democracy and serve the interests of Swiss politicians, civil servants and diplomats more than the rest of the country. It is hard to argue with these contentions.

Blocking referendums are a check on the ambitions of the political class: a guarantee that a party with a transient majority cannot make major changes without popular consent. Properly used, they detract very little from parliamentary supremacy, and add a good deal to Parliament's popularity and legitimacy. We propose the following process:

1. After a Bill has received its Third Reading, but before it receives Royal Assent, there will be a seven-day period in which any British citizen who is registered to vote may submit a written objection to the Clerk to the House of Commons, together with a deposit and an administration fee. To prevent the clogging up of the system with cranky objections there should be a requirement for a minimum number of signatures at this stage: perhaps 20,000.

2. Within the next 20 days, the Clerk shall determine the text of the petition and subsequent referendum. Again as in New Zealand, the Clerk may consult the public about the precise wording. The Clerk must ensure that there can only be two answers to the referendum question: 'yes' to approve the legislation or 'no' to reject it.

3. The petitioner shall then have 100 days to collect the necessary signatures. The threshold should be high enough to deter frivolous challenges, but not so high as to be prohibitive. In Switzerland, the figure is 2.5 per cent of the electorate, a figure also advocated by the British campaign group Our Say. Again, signatures could be collected online as well as conventionally, with petitioners providing names and addresses. The sole stipulation would be that every petitioner be a registered voter and a British national.

4. Once the Clerk rules that the petition is valid, it is formally presented to the House of Commons (traditionalists might be reassured to know that there has been a formal mechanism for petitioning the House since the sixteenth century). The Government may at this stage withdraw the Bill.

5. If the Bill is not withdrawn, the Government must name a date for the referendum within 100 days. A Bill that fails to secure public support automatically lapses. (Conversely, one that is carried gains considerably enhanced authority.)

Veto referendums are triggered only rarely in the states which provide for them. The very fact of their existence is enough to concentrate the minds of parliamentarians and to reduce the volume of legislation. And, while the check is small-c conservative, in the literal sense that it tends to preserve the *status quo*, it is also small-l liberal in the sense that it is often a check on illiberal and draconian measures.

Automatic referendums
There is one field of policy where we suggest that referendums be triggered automatically: constitutional change.

The rationale is that politicians elected under one set of rules ought not to be able to alter those rules without a further and explicit mandate. To take an extreme example, there is at present no formal mechanism to prevent MPs voting to extend the life of the current Parliament to 20 or 50 years. If MPs want to vary the period between elections – something they have done several times over the years – it seems only fair to require them to put such a change to the people for direct endorsement.

By the same token, any changes in the voting system – a move to proportional representation, for example – should trigger a referendum. So should a move to unicameralism, or an alteration of the composition of the Upper House. And so should a major shift in the locus of power: reversing Scottish devolution, say, or transferring more power to the EU.

Who is to decide what constitutes such a change? How are we to distinguish between, say, regular constituency boundary redistributions to keep up with demographic change (which most people would accept should not require a referendum) and a move to multi-member constituencies based on an Alternative Vote system (which would have major consequences for the various parties)? We have no constitutional court, no external authority higher than the Crown-in-Parliament.

Such decisions should be made by the Attorney General, as in Ireland. There is no reason to believe that the holder of this office would not discharge it properly and impartially. But, in the event that people felt that a major constitutional change was being pushed through without a mandate, they would always have the option of petitioning for a blocking referendum.

Local referendums
Perhaps the most practical benefit of the referendum is as a test of local opinion. Exactly the same mechanisms outlined above could be translated to local level: the right of popular initiative (proposals forced on to the council's agenda having attracted sufficient signatures); the blocking referendum (again, provided it attracted sufficient support); and the constitutional referendum (if two authorities wished to merge, for example, or if councillors wanted to change the electoral system by which they were elected).

Local referendums are already part of life in England and Wales. The 2000 Local Government Act allowed for referendums on directly elected mayors, and 35 have so far been held. There have also been local plebiscites on raising council tax in order to pay for specific services (so far, these have always been rejected). There has also been one referendum on ending a school's selective status (also rejected).

It is tempting simply to duplicate the legislation at local level, even down to the 2.5 per cent threshold for a veto referendum. But, in accordance with localist principles, we would rather give the option to local councils to adopt such legislation, and to adapt it to local conditions.

In any event, the mere possibility of local referendums should serve tangibly and immediately to improve the performance of local councils.

Part Three
The 30 steps

Books of this kind are often a wish-list of proposals, some practical, some fantastical. This one is different. There is nothing we have proposed that could not be implemented swiftly, provided there be political will.

To prove this point, and to assist any incoming government that is attracted to our manifesto, we have indicated how our agenda might take legislative force. What follows is a list of the various legal acts that would be needed to implement our programme. Some of what we propose could be effected by an Order in Council, or by a simple executive decision. Some, especially the parts dealing with the internal reform of Parliament, will need only Motions of the House. But the bulk will require primary legislation.

What follows is not the proposed text of Bills themselves: that is a task for specialised parliamentary officials. We have, however, sought to give some indication of the full ramifications of our agenda, including the requisite repeal of previous legislation.

There are 30 separate steps. Allowing time for superfluous business, for emergency debates and for unforeseen events – as well, obviously, as parliamentary recesses – we believe they could all be in force within 12 months. The changes we propose are simply stated and could be quickly delivered. Their effect will be to restore Britain's body politic to health.

1. Abolish MPs' perks

A Resolution of the House of Commons that would scrap MPs perks:

Notwithstanding Resolutions of the House of 20 December 1971, 5 July 2001, 28 March 2007, 3 July 2008, and any provision in other Resolutions relating thereto, the Communications Allowance and the Additional Costs Allowance shall be abolished with immediate effect.

2. MPs to be bound by the same laws as everyone else

A Bill to make provision about the application of legislation to Parliament; and for connected purposes.

1 *Legislation to apply to Parliament*
  (1) *The presumption that legislation does not apply to Parliament unless it contains express provision to that effect is abolished.*
  (2) *Any enactment which—*
    (a) *extends to England and Wales, and*
    (b) *is in force on the day on which this Act comes into force, or*
    (c) *has been enacted before that day but comes into force after that day,*
    shall apply to Parliament.
  (3) *Subsection (2) has effect subject to section 2.*
  (4) *In this section—*
    "enactment" means an Act of Parliament or a statutory instrument; and
    "enacted" means passed (in the case of an Act of Parliament) or made (in the case of a statutory instrument).
2 *Saving for freedom of speech in Parliament*

Nothing in this Act—

    (a)   affects Article IX of the Bill of Rights 1689, or

    (b)   detracts in any way from the privilege of freedom of speech in Parliament.

3   Short title and commencement

    (1)   This Act may be cited as the Parliament (Application of Legislation) Act 2008.

    (2)   This Act comes into force at the end of two months beginning with the day it is passed.

3. Elect the House of Commons Speaker by secret ballot

An amendment to the Standing Orders as follows:

Standing Order 1A (Re-election of Former Speaker) be repealed
Standing Order 1B (Election of Speaker by Secret Ballot) be amended by leaving out paragraph 1 and inserting 'On any occasion when it is necessary to proceed with the choice of a Speaker, the election shall be by secret ballot.'

4. Confirm Crown appointments of senior Commons Clerks

Those letters patent-issued with regard to the appointment the Under Clerk of the Parliaments (and who is customarily referred to as the Clerk of the House of Commons) would be issued only after a motion approving the appointment by the House.

5. Elect select committee chairmen

A new Standing Order, as follows:

1) *On any occasion when it is necessary to proceed with the choice of a new Select Committee Chairman, the election shall be by secret ballot.*

2) *Preparatory arrangements for a ballot shall be made under the supervision of the Clerk of the House.*

3a) *Nominations of candidates shall be in writing to the Clerk of the House within the first seven days of each new Parliament, or within a fortnight of an incumbent vacating the Chair for whatever reason.*

3b) *Each nomination shall consist of a signed statement made by the candidate declaring his willingness to stand for election accompanied by the signatures of not fewer than twelve Members, of whom not fewer than three shall be Members elected to the House as members of any party other than that to which the candidate belongs.*

4) *If only one Member is nominated, the Speaker shall invite the Member to submit himself to the House, and shall then put forthwith the question that that Member do take the Chair of the said Committee.*

5) *If two or more Members are nominated, an election shall be held in accordance with paragraphs 6 to 12 below:*

6) *When the House meets, the order in which candidates may address the House shall be determined by lot; the Speaker shall then invite each candidate to address the House; and after all candidates have been given an opportunity to speak, the Speaker shall direct the House to proceed to a ballot.*

7) *Each Member intending to vote shall be provided with a ballot paper bearing the names of the candidates listed in alphabetical order. Each such member may only vote for one candidate on the ballot paper.*

8) *As soon as practicable after the votes have been counted the Speaker shall announce to the House the number of votes cast for each candidate.*

9) *If a candidate has received more than half the votes cast in a ballot, the Speaker shall forthwith put the question that that Member do take the Chairmanship of the said committee.*

10) *If no candidate has received more than half the votes cast in a ballot the Speaker shall direct the House to proceed forthwith to a further ballot.*

11) *In any further ballot no new nominations may be received, and the name of the candidate who received the fewest votes in the previous ballot shall be removed from the ballot paper.*

12) *In the event of a tie at any stage in the ballot process, the Speaker shall have the casting vote.*

13) *Once the Chairman has been elected, the House shall nominate the other members of the Committee as provided for by Standing Order 121 (Nomination of select committees).*

6. Parliamentary committee hearings to appoint the heads of non-departmental public bodies

An amendment to the Public Appointments Order in Council 2002:

The Commissioner shall not recommend any candidate be appointed head of any non-departmental public body whose nomination has not been considered and approved by the relevant select committee of the House of Commons. At the discretion of the select committee Chairman, such candidates for approval may be requested to appear before the committee in either public or private.

The Public Appointment Commissioner's Code of Practice (clauses 2.04 to 3.36 covering all ministerial appointments of chief executives of non-departmental public bodies) and principles, amended:

THE PRINCIPLES
1) *Ministerial responsibility*
    Responsibility for nominating candidates is with ministers.
2) *Merit*
    All such nominations must be made with regard to the overriding

principle of selection based on merit, by the well-informed choice of individuals who through their abilities, experience and qualities match the need of the public body in question.

3) **Parliamentary scrutiny**
   No appointment will take place without first being approved by the relevant select committee of the House of Commons. At the discretion of the select committee Chairman, candidates nominated by ministers and others may be requested to appear before the committee in either public or private.

4) **Probity, openness and transparency**
   Chief executives must perform their duties with integrity. The principles of open government must be applied to the appointments process, its working must be transparent and information provided about the appointments made.

7. Parliamentary committee hearings to appoint Permanent Under Secretaries of State and the heads of Executive Agencies

An amendment to the Civil Service Order in Council 1995 and the Ministers of the Crown Act 1975:

Civil Service Order in Council 1995.
The Commissioner's approval for appointment, insert as new 5(4):
The Commissioner shall not recommend any candidate be appointed Permanent Secretary, or as head of any Executive Agency, whose nomination has not been considered and approved by the relevant select committee of the House of Commons. At the discretion of the select committee Chairman, such candidates for approval may be requested to appear before the committee in either public or private.

The Civil Service Commissioners recruitment code be amended accordingly.

Ministers of the Crown Act 1975.
Amend Section 1 of the Ministers of the Crown Act 1975 so that functions
previously exercisable by a Minister of the Crown may not be transferred
to another Minister of the Crown without a vote by Parliament.

8. Annualised budgets for non-departmental public bodies

A Bill that would ensure Parliament had direct oversight over quango expenditure and amendments to certain Standing Orders:

> *The Bill would amend each Act or secondary enactment establishing all*
> *non-departmental public bodies (Executive, Advisory, Tribunal and*
> *Independent Monitoring bodies) so as the Secretary for State shall fund*
> *non-departmental public bodies from monies, including grant-in-aid,*
> *voted by Parliament, subject to the approval of the relevant select committee*
> *of the House of Commons.*
> *The Secretary of State shall not release to such public bodies monies voted*
> *by Parliament until such time as the relevant select committee of the House*
> *of Commons has voted to approve that the Secretary of State do so. At the*
> *discretion of the select committee Chairman, Ministers and the accounting*
> *officers of such public bodies may be required to appear before the*
> *committee in either public or private.*
> *Amendments, where relevant, to Standing Orders 48 to 56 (Public Money)*
> *and 121 to 152 (Select Committees) to allow such select committee*
> *hearings to take place.*

9. Scrap state subsidised political broadcasts for political parties

An amendment to the Political Parties, Elections and Referendums Act 2000 to repeal sections 11 and 36 and inserting a new section:

Party political broadcasts

1) *A broadcaster shall not include in its broadcasting services any party political broadcast other than a paid advertisement.*

2) *In this Act 'broadcaster' means:-*

   (a) *the holder of a licence under the Broadcasting Act 1990 or 1996,*

   (b) *the British Broadcasting Corporation, or*

   (c) *Sianel Pedwar Cymru*

and repealing section 333 of the Communications Act 2003.

10. Scrap state-funded electioneering for political parties

An amendment to the Representation of the People Act 1983 in order to repeal section 91 (Candidate's right to send election address post free) and inserting a new section in the Political Parties, Elections and Referendums Act 2000:

Distribution of election material

1) *The Post Office may not distribute any election material except at the expense of the promoter of the material.*

2) *In this section 'election material' and 'the promoter' have the same meaning as in section 143.*

11. Scrap use of public money for political parties

Revoking resolutions of the House of Commons of 26 May 1999 relating to Opposition Parties (Financial Assistance), and of 28 March 2007 relating to the Communications Allowance; and by amending the Political Parties, Elections and Referendums Act 2000 to state that no financial support shall be provided for party political activity out of money provided by Parliament.

12. Require all donations of over £1,000 to be registered

An amendment to the Political Parties, Elections and Referendums Act 2000 so as to:

1)   *Section 62 of the 2000 Act (quarterly donation reports) is amended as follows.*

2)   *In each of subsections (4) (a), (4) (b) and (5) (b) for '£5,000' substitute '£1,000'.*

3)   *Omit subsections (6), (6A) and (7).*

4)   *In subsection (8) for 'subsections (4) to (7)' in each place where they occur substitute 'subsections (4) and (5)'.*

5)   *In subsection (11) omit paragraph (b) and the word 'but' immediately preceding it.*

6)   *In paragraph (12):-*
   (a)   for '(7)' substitute '(5)', and
   (b)   in paragraph (b) omit 'or (6)'.

7)   *Section 63 of the 2000 Act (weekly donation reports during general election periods) is amended as follows.*

8)   *In subsection (3) for '£5,000' substitute '£1,000'.*

13. A smaller ministerial payroll

An amendment to the Ministerial and other Salaries Act 1975 to reduce the number of MPs on the ministerial payroll from 83 to 40 by substituting '83' in paragraph 2(c) of Schedule 1 with '40'.

14. Open primaries

A Bill amending the Representation of the People Act 1983, the Political Parties, Elections and Referendum Act 2000 and other enactments:

Insert into the Representation of the People Act 1983 clauses within Part IV Special Provisions as to other local elections, clauses requiring that 'Where one or more registered political party requests it, there shall be a primary election of all those entitled to vote'.

Registered political parties able request primary elections shall be as defined in Part II of the Political Parties, Elections and Referendum Act 2000.

Entitlement to vote in primary elections shall be as outlined in section 1 of the Representation of the People Act 1983 concerning Parliamentary elections.

The conduct and the place and manner of voting shall be as that prescribed for local elections in Section 18 and 23 of the Representation of the People Act 1983 concerning Parliamentary elections.

The role of the Returning Office shall be as that outlined in Section 23 of the Representation of the People Act 1983 concerning Parliamentary elections.

Registered political parties requesting to take part in primary elections shall meet the expenses incurred by the Returning Officer in conducting the primary election, as set out in section 29 of the Representation of the People Act 1983 regarding payments by and to returning officer and subsequent enactments.

Section 135 of the Political Parties, Elections and Referendum Act 2000 shall be amended in order to define candidates in primary elections as:

A person becomes a candidate at a primary election on the last day for publication of notice of the election if on or before that day he is declared by his registered party as one of no more than six nominated candidates at the election.

15. Sheriff Bill

A Bill to provide for the replacement of police authorities with elected sheriffs; to make provision regarding the duties and powers of sheriffs; and for connected purposes.

1   *Replacement of police authorities with sheriffs*

    (1)   *There shall be a sheriff for each police area listed in Schedule 1 to the Police Act 1996 (c. 16).*

    (2)   *Each sheriff shall be elected in accordance with section 2.*

    (3)   *Each police authority shall be abolished on the day after the first election of a sheriff for the police area for which it is responsible.*

2   *Election of a sheriff*

    (1)   *The Secretary of State may by regulations make provision for the election of a sheriff in each police area every four years.*

    (2)   *The voting system to be used for the elections shall be the simple majority system.*

    (3)   *Regulations made under this section shall include provision about-*

        (a)   *the designation of the local authorities which are to be responsible for holding the elections;*

        (b)   *the timing and conduct of the elections;*

        (c)   *eligibility to stand for election; and*

        (d)   *eligibility to vote in the elections.*

3   *Duties of the sheriff*

    (1)   *Every sheriff shall secure the maintenance of an efficient and effective police force for the police area.*

    (2)   *In particular, the sheriff shall have responsibility for-*

        (a)   *holding the police budget and determining how much council tax should be raised for policing;*

        (b)   *the appointment and dismissal of the chief constable;*

        (c)   *the setting of local police priorities and performance targets;*

        (d)   *monitoring the performance of the police force against targets set;*

        (e)   *overseeing complaints against the police; and*

        (f) overseeing the work of the crown prosecutor in the police   area.

(3)   *In pursuance of subsection (2)(a), all police grants previously payable to police authorities under section 46 of the Police Act 1996 shall be payable to the sheriff.*

(4)   *The local authority responsible for holding the election of a sheriff under section 2 shall have a duty to provide the sheriff with-*

    (a)   *such remuneration and expenses as it considers appropriate; and*

    (b)   *such staff and resources as it considers appropriate to enable the sheriff to discharge his functions.*

4   Local policing plans

(1)   *The sheriff shall, before the beginning of each financial year, issue a plan setting out the proposed arrangements for the policing of the area during the year (the local policing plan).*

(2)   *The local policing plan shall provide information on how the duties set out in section 3 will be discharged, and shall include a statement of the sheriff's priorities for the year, of the financial resources expected to be available and of the proposed allocation of those resources.*

(3)   *The sheriff must consult the chief constable of the police area before issuing a local policing plan and have regard to his views.*

(4)   *The sheriff may take such steps as he considers appropriate to consult local people before issuing the local policing plan.*

(5)   *The sheriff shall arrange for every local policing plan issued under this section to be published in such manner as appears to him to be appropriate, and shall send a copy of the plan to the Secretary of State.*

5   Annual report by sheriff

(1)   *As soon as possible after the end of each financial year every sheriff shall issue a report relating to the policing of the police area for the year.*

(2)   *A report issued by a sheriff under this section for any year shall include an assessment of the extent to which the local policing plan for that year issued under section 4 has been carried out.*

(3)   *A sheriff shall arrange for every report issued by him under this section to be published in such manner as appears to him to be appropriate, and shall send a copy of the report to the Secretary of State.*

6   General functions of chief constables

(1)   *A police force shall be under the direction and control of the chief constable.*

(2)   *In discharging his functions, every chief constable shall have regard to the local   policing plan issued by the sheriff for his police area under section 4.*

7   Oversight of criminal proceedings

(1)   *In pursuance of his duties under section 3(2)(f), a sheriff may require-*

   (a)   *the chief constable of his police area, and*

   (b)   *the crown prosecutor with responsibility for his police area,*

       to provide such information as he wishes regarding any case or cases.

(2)   *Chief constables and crown prosecutors must provide to the sheriff any information requested under subsection (1) in a timely manner.*

(3)   *Following the provision of information under subsection (2), a sheriff may, if in his view he has good reason for doing so, give instruction to the crown prosecutor-*

   (a)   *not to institute proceedings, or*

   (b)   *to discontinue proceedings,*

       in any case being considered by the crown prosecutor.

(4)   *A crown prosecutor must comply with any instruction given under subsection (3).*

8   Consequential amendments and regulations

(1)   *The Secretary of State may by regulations make any amendments, repeals and revocations necessary to implement the provisions of this Act.*

(2)   *The power to make orders and regulations under this Act is exercisable by statutory instrument.*

(3)   *A statutory instrument containing regulations made under this Act is subject to annulment in pursuance of a resolution of either House of Parliament.*

9   **Expenses**
There shall be paid out of money provided by Parliament-

(a)   *any sums payable to be paid by the Secretary of State for or in connection with the carrying out of his functions under this Act; and*

(b)   *any increase attributable to this Act in the sums which are payable out of money so provided under any other Act.*

10   **Short title, commencement and extent**

(1)   *This Act may be cited as the Police (Elected Sheriffs) Act 2008.*

(2)   *This Act shall come into force 12 months after the date on which it is passed.*

(3)   *This Act extends to England and Wales only.*

16. Scrap the Human Rights Act 1998

A Bill to repeal the Human Rights Act, along with all subsequent enactments, including the Human Rights (Amendment) Order 2004 and Human Rights Act (Amendment) Order 2005.

17. Withdraw from the European Convention on Human Rights

This can be done under Crown Prerogative powers, with no need for legislation.

18. Reserve powers

A Bill to guarantee the supremacy of Parliament against foreign treaties and domestic judicial activism:

Repeal the European Communities Act 1972, and include the following clause:

> *Notwithstanding any provision of the European Communities Act 1972 or any subsequent enactments or rulings by any United Kingdom court, nothing shall affect or be construed by any court in the United Kingdom as affecting the supremacy of the United Kingdom Parliament.*

Abolish Royal Prerogative with regard to the power to enter into treaties and conventions by stating that:

> *No international treaty or convention entered into by any government shall receive Royal Assent until the House of Commons has voted to approve the said international treaty or convention.*
>
> *The House of Commons shall vote to approve any advice given by Ministers to Her Majesty with regard to all treaty making and powers of Royal Prerogative exercised by the Crown.*

Require a referendum on any International Treaties and convention that would affect the supremacy of the United Kingdom Parliament with the following clause:

> *No international treaty or convention so approved by the House of Commons that shall affect or be construed by any court in the United Kingdom as affecting the supremacy of the United Kingdom Parliament, shall receive Royal Assent without a popular referendum.*

Curtail the scope for judicial activism on the basis of international treaties and conventions with the following clause:

No international treaty or convention shall form the basis on which any court in the United Kingdom may adjudicate, unless and until the House of Commons has explicitly voted that United Kingdom courts may do so.

19. Appoint senior judges through parliamentary hearings

A Bill to amend the Constitutional Reform Act 2005 and other related enactments:

Repeal sections 61, 62, 64, 65 and 66 of the Constitutional Reform Act 2005.

Each of those powers and provisions in the 2005 Act relating to the appointment of judges be transferred from the Judicial Appointments Commission to the Lord Chancellor, subject to Part 4 below.
Each of those powers and provisions in the 2005 Act relating to the judiciary be transferred from the Judicial Appointments and Conduct Ombudsman to the Lord Chancellor.

Part 4 of the Constitutional Reform Act 2005 be amended in order that:

1) *No judicial appointment made by the Lord Chancellor under Part 3 above can take effect without a vote by the House of Commons, or a Committee of the House of Commons, to ratify the appointment.*

2) *A Committee of the House of Commons established to review judicial appointments may hold confirmation hearings. Such hearings may be held in public and enable the committee to scrutinise the appointments made by the Lord Chancellor; members of the committee may request that appointees attend such hearings and answer questions; after such hearings a vote be held to confirm the appointment made by the Lord Chancellor.*

3) *Any appointee as Lord Chancellor be subject to a vote by the House of Commons, or a Committee of the House of Commons.*

Miscellaneous and general. The Constitutional Reform Act 2005 and other enactments be amended in accordance with Part 1 to 4 above.

20. Parents' Freedom Bill

A Bill to give parents a new legal right over their children's education:

Establish a legal right for parents.

> *Every parent, and/or legal guardian with a child of primary or secondary school age shall have the right to request and receive control over their child's budget, as defined in Part 2 below.*
>
> *A parent, and/or legal guardian, who has indicated in writing to their Local Education Authority that they wish to have control over their child's budget, before 1 August each year, shall be granted control over their child's budget by 1 September that year.*

Establish the child's budget.

> 1) *A 'child's budget' for each school year is the school's budget defined in 2) below, divided by the total number of children of that year group living within the Local Education Authority attending local authority-maintained schools.*
>
> 2) *Each Local Education Authority's 'schools budget' for the school year is the amount appropriated by the authority for meeting all expenditure by the authority in that year for the purposes of education, as well as any other expenditure made either directly by the Secretary of State or any other money provided by Parliament, including any capital expenditure. The schools budget for each Local Education Authority shall include all indirect actual expenditure, including administration costs not necessarily spent directly on local schools.*

Give parents control over the budget.

1) *Each Local Education Authority shall have a responsibility to ensure that each parent and/or legal guardian resident locally, who has indicated in writing by 1 August that they wish to control their budget, shall be able to determine which school receives their child's budget.*

2) *Every parent granted control over their child's budget shall be able to allocate the budget in its entirety to any local authority-maintained school or other recognized school in the country willing to offer their child a place, in order to fund their child's education for that year.*

3) *Where a parent and/or legal guardian wishes to transfer his child from one school to another, he may request that the school reimburse his local authority, in order to allow the child's budget for any outstanding terms of the education year to be transferred to a different school willing to accept the child.*

Parts 1, 2 and 3 above will require appropriate amendments to the Education Act 1986, Education Reform Act 1988, Education Act 1994, Education Act 1996, Education Act 1997, Education Act 2002, Education Act 2005 and Education and Inspections Act 2006.

21. Schools' Freedom Bill

A Bill to make every school independent so as to:

Allow schools to acquire the status of 'free schools'.

1) *Any school where the governing body votes by a simple majority to do so may write to the Local Education Authority before 1 August each year indicating that the school wishes to gain 'free school' status under the provisions of this Act.*

2) *'Free schools' shall continue to receive funding from Local Education Authorities; they shall continue to receive funding at the direction*

of the Secretary of State and other monies provided by Parliament; they shall be able to receive funds via child's budgets.

Abolish the national curriculum.

'Free schools' shall be exempt from the following:
1)   *Those sections of the Education Reform Act 1988, the Education Act 1997, Education Act 2002 and other enactments relating to the national curriculum. Free schools shall have no need to have regard to the body corporate known as the Qualifications and Curriculum Authority nor its functions as set out in Part 5 of the Education Act 1997 with regard to a national curriculum.*
2)   *Parts 6 and 7 of the Education Act 2002 and all other enactments relating to the national curriculum.*

Abolish national testing and assessment.

'Free schools' shall be exempt from the following:
1)   *Those sections of the Education Reform Act 1988, the Education Act 1997 and other enactments relating to national testing and assessment. Free schools shall have no need to have regard to the body corporate know as the Qualifications and Curriculum Authority or its functions as set out in Part 5 of the Education Act 1997 with regard to school examination and assessment.*
2)   *Part 4 of the Education Act 1997 and all other enactments relating to national assessment and testing.*

Allow free schools to run their own affairs with regard to discipline, admissions and staff.

'Free schools' shall be exempt from the following:
1)   *Those sections of the Education Act 1997 and all other enactments relating to school discipline. The governing bodies of free schools shall determine the schools own standards of behaviour and*

conduct; they shall be able to enter into 'home/school agreements' with parents of children attending the school, setting out reasonable standards of expected behaviour and conduct. Free schools shall publish their admissions criteria annually, making such criteria available publicly.

2) *Part 3 of the Education Act 1997 and all other enactments relating to school admissions. The governing bodies of free schools shall determine each school's own admissions criteria; they shall publish their admissions criteria annually, making such criteria available publicly.*

3) *Part 8 of the Education Act 2002. Free schools shall be able to determine pay and conditions without regard to the School Teachers' Review Body or other clauses of the Act relating to the employment of staff.*

Further changes will be required to the Education Act 1986, Education Reform Act 1988, Education Act 1994, Education Act 1996, Education Act 1997, Education Act 2002, Education Act 2005 and Education and Inspections Act 2006.

22. Localism Bill

A Bill to devolve power to local authorities:

Devolve those functions and competences given to the Scottish Executive within Part II of the Scotland Act 1998 to metropolitan county councils, non-metropolitan county councils and the London Assembly in England and Wales.

Devolve those powers given to the Scottish Parliament within Part I of the Scotland Act 1998 to metropolitan county councils, non-metropolitan county councils and the London Assembly in England and Wales.

Confer on metropolitan county councils, non-metropolitan county councils and the London Assembly in England and Wales certain tax-raising powers.

Maintain as Reserved Matters for the Parliament of the United Kingdom those areas set out in Schedule 5 of the Scotland Act 1998.

Repeal the Secretary of State for Communities and Local Government Order 2006 (Statutory Instrument 2006 No. 1926) and abolish the Department for Communities and Local Government. Such powers exercised by the Secretary of State at the Department of Communities and Local Government to principle local authorities in England and Wales with regard to:

- *Planning*
- *Building regulations*
- *Civil resilience*
- *Fire and fire services*
- *Homelessness*
- *Housing*
- *Neighbourhood renewal*
- *Social exclusion*
- *Sustainable communities*
- *Urban policy*
- *Community cohesion*

23. Set councils free

A Bill to make local government largely self-financing:

Amend the Local Government Financial Settlement such that ring-fenced grants (including narrow and broad ring-fenced and targeted grants) made to metropolitan county authorities, non-metropolitan authorities, unitary authorities, district authorities and the London Assembly shall be rolled into the Formula Grant allocated to each such local authority.

Amend the Local Government Finance Act 1992 and subsequent enactments in order that metropolitan county authorities, non-metropolitan authorities, unitary authorities and the Greater London

Authority shall set local Non-Domestic Rates in accordance with Part III of the Local Government Finance Act 1988.

Amend the Local Government Finance Act 1988, Finance Act 1990, Local Government Finance Act 1992, Value Added Tax Act 1994 and other relevant enactments in order that:

The Formula Grant awarded to each metropolitan county authority, non-metropolitan authority, unitary authority, and the Greater London Authority shall be funded out of revenue collected from VAT.

Metropolitan county authorities, non-metropolitan authorities, unitary authorities, and the Greater London Authority shall be deemed as 'billing authorities' for the purposes of collecting VAT and made responsible for collecting VAT.

Billing authorities shall be able to retain such VAT collected, and the size of the Formula Grant they receive shall then be reduced by the amount of VAT thus collected.

VAT charged at each stage of the transaction process shall thereafter be converted into the charge only at the point of retail, a Local Sales Tax.

Billing authorities shall be allowed to set their own rate for the Local Sales Tax.

The Local Government Financial Settlement shall continue to allocate an outstanding Formula Grant and in so doing shall have regard to the need to ensure a measure of revenue equalisation between different billing authorities.

24. Healthcare

A Bill to amend the Health and Social Care Act 2001, the National Health Service Act 2006 and other enactments so as to:

Maintain those provisions within the National Health Service Act 2006 Section 1 that guarantee that those who decide not to opt out by creating an individual health account shall continue to be provided with health services free of charge.

Amend Part 9 of the National Health Service Act 2006 and other enactments to allow individuals to create 'individual health accounts'.

Amend the Health and Social Care Act 2001, the National Health Service Act 2006 and other enactments to allow individual National Insurance contributions to be used to pay for services and treatments otherwise provided for under Section 1 of the National Health Service Act 2006.

Amend the National Insurance Contributions Act 2002 and other enactments in order to allow individual National Insurance contributions to be paid directly into individual health accounts. Amendments shall also permit additional contributions to be paid into such accounts on top of National Insurance contributions.

Amend the National Health Service Act 2006 to require the Secretary of State to maintain a schedule within the Act defining those treatments and health services to be regarded as 'standard health care services' and other 'critical illness treatments'.

25. Local welfare

A Bill to amend the Social Security Administration Act 1992, the Welfare Reform and Pensions Act 1999 and the Welfare Reform Act 2007 in order to require the following:

Part 2 of the Social Security Administration Act 1992 and subsequent enactments be amended so that those powers of adjudication with regard to benefits conferred on the Secretary of State in the Act shall be passed to the relevant cabinet portfolio holder within each metropolitan county authority, non-metropolitan authority, unitary authority, and the Greater London Authority.

Part 2 of the Social Security Administration Act 1992 and subsequent enactments be amended so that those questions currently determined by the Secretary of State with regard to benefit entitlement shall be passed to the relevant cabinet portfolio holder within each metropolitan county authority, non-metropolitan authority, unitary authority, and the Greater London Authority.

Part 1 of the Welfare Reform Act 2007 and subsequent enactments regarding Employment and Support Allowance be amended so that responsibility for determining assessment criteria and managing the 'assessment phase' shall be devolved from the Secretary of State to the relevant cabinet portfolio holder within each metropolitan county authority, non-metropolitan authority, unitary authority, and the Greater London Authority.

Part 2 of the Welfare Reform Act 2007 and subsequent enactments regarding Housing Benefit and Council Tax Benefit be amended so that responsibility for assessment criteria and eligibility shall be devolved from the Secretary of State to the relevant cabinet portfolio holder within each metropolitan county authority, non-metropolitan authority, unitary authority, and the Greater London Authority.

Amendments within the Social Security Administration Act 1992, the Welfare Reform and Pensions Act 1999, the Welfare Reform Act 2007 and other enactments in order to devolve oversight of budgets for Employment and Support Allowance, Housing Benefit, Council Tax Benefit and other benefits, be devolved by the Secretary of State to each metropolitan county authority, non-metropolitan authority, unitary authority, and the Greater London Authority.

26. The Great Repeal Bill

A Bill to repeal:

1. *Legislative and Regulatory Reform Act 2006*

2. *Employment Act 2002 (Chapter 1 of Part 1 of Schedule 2 and paragraphs 6 and 9 of Schedule 2) and the Employment Act 2002 (Dispute Resolution) Regulations 2004 SI 2004/752.*

3. *Statutory instruments and regulations enacted under European Works Council Directive rules and European Social Chapter enactments.*

4. *Part-time Workers (Prevention of Less Favourable Treatment) Regulations 2000 (SI 2000/1551) and 2002 (SI 2002/2035).*

5. *Sections of the Weights and Measures Act 1985, and various secondary legislation, including the Weights and Measures*

(Packaged Goods) Regulations 2006 (SI 2006/659), which require retailers to use certain weights and measurements rather than others.

6. *Sections of the 2004 Housing Act that require Home Information Packs to be used.*

7. *Statutory Instrument 2005 No. 1011 under the Companies Act 1985 relating to financial reviews and directors' reports.*

8. *Money laundering regulations, including Statutory Instruments 2007 No. 2157, 2007 No. 3299, 2006 No. 308, 2006 No. 1070, 2003 No. 171, 2003 No. 3075, 2001 No. 1819 and 2001 No. 3641.*

9. *Sections of the secondary legislation enacted over the past decade under the 1974 Health and Safety at Work Act.*

10. *Regulatory Reform (Fire Safety) Order 2005 Statutory Instrument 1541.*

11. *Sections of the Local Government Act 2000 that established a Standards Boards to oversee the conduct of locally elected councillors.*

12. *Sections of the Local Government Act 1999 that dictate Best Value rules for local government.*

13. *Requirements for Comprehensive Performance Assessments on local councils.*

14. *Regional Development Agencies Act 1998 and earlier legislation establishing Government Regional Offices.*

15. *Sections of the Police Act 1997 relating to the establishment of the Criminal Records Bureau, and all subsequent requirements for voluntary groups and organisations to use it.*

16. *Safeguarding Vulnerable Groups Act 2006 which established the Independent Safeguarding Authority.*

17. *Identity Cards Act 2006.*

18. *Sections 60 to 62 of the Countryside and Rights of Way Act 2002.*

19. *Hunting Act 2004.*

20. *Regulation of Investigatory Powers Act 2000 and abolish the Surveillance Commissioners.*

21. *Amend the Police and Criminal Evidence Act 1984 to allow police officers, accountable to a locally elected Sheriff and the courts, freedom to get on with their job.*
22. *Gambling Act 2005.*
23. *Dangerous Dogs Act 1989.*
24. *Football Spectators Act 1989.*
25. *War Crimes Act 1991.*
26. *Firearms Act 1998.*
27. *European Communities Act 1972.*

27. Parliamentary committee hearings to appoint Heads of Mission, Ambassadors and High Commissioners

An amendment to the Diplomatic Service Order in Council 1991:

Insert after 3 (1):
The Commissioners shall not give such written approval with regard to any appointment of any Head of Mission, Ambassador, High Commissioner, or United Kingdom Permanent Representative, without the approval of the House of Commons Foreign Affairs select committee. At the discretion of the select committee Chairman, such persons may appear before the committee in either public or private.
The Commissioners recruitment code be amended accordingly.

28. Parliament to control trade policy

A Bill to reform trade policy:

Repeal the Import and Export Control Act 1990 and the Export Control Act 2002.

Remove the powers of the Secretary of State to issue export control orders.
Repeal the Import and Export Control Act 1990, the Export Control Act
2002 and subsequent statutory instruments.
Remove all excise duties, tariffs and other such charges levied on the import
of goods into the United Kingdom, or for services provided on 1 January
the following year.
Create a 'reserve list' of nations with whom trade could be restricted or controlled
or subject to export controls, but not tariffs or charges, by the Secretary of State
in the interests of national security, subject to approval by the House of Commons.

29. Direct democracy – local

A Bill that would allow citizens to trigger referendums and initiative
measures at a local level:

DIRECT DEMOCRACY BILL
Part 1. Local authority electors
1)   *Electors' right to referendum*
    (1)   *A minimum 100 electors may within seven working days of a*
decision ('the initial decision') being made by a local authority
lodge an 'intention to raise a petition' at the offices of a local
authority to prevent the authority from acting upon that decision.
    (2)   *When an intention to raise a petition has been lodged in*
accordance with subsection (1) the local authority must
reconsider the decision and may not implement the decision
until it has done so.
    (3)   *Where a local authority has reconsidered a decision*
pursuant to subsection (2) and has decided to approve the
decision the electors may within three months of the initial
decision being taken lodge a petition at the offices of the
authority signed by not less than 2.5 per cent of electors
calling for a referendum on the decision.

    (4)   *Where a petition signed by 2.5 per cent of the electors has been duly lodged, the authority*

        (a)   *shall organise a referendum of all its electors on the decision in question; and*

        (b)   *shall not act on the decision in question until a referendum has been held pursuant to this subsection and has failed to secure a majority of those voting in favour of preventing the authority from acting on its decision.*

  2)   *Electors' right to raise agenda item*

    (1)   *No less than 2.5 per cent of electors of a local authority may by petition, at any time, require a meeting of that authority as soon as is practicable to consider or reconsider as the case may be*

        (a)   *any policy made or decision taken by that authority or any committee or subcommittee of the authority;*

        (b)   *any new policy provided that the proposed policy is within the competence of the authority;*

        (c)   *seeking new powers for the authority which may include the transfer of any powers from any other body provided that no such requirement may be made more than once in any 12-month period.*

30. Direct democracy – national

A Bill that would allow citizens to trigger referendums and initiate legislation nationally:

DIRECT DEMOCRACY BILL
Part 2. UK Parliament electors
  3)   *Electors' right to referendum*

    (1)   *Not less than of 2.5 per cent of electors*

        (a)   *enrolled as eligible to vote at the previous parliamentary election; and*

(b)   covered by the extent of any Act or Regulations made
         by Parliament

may within six months of the passing of that Act or the
making of those Regulations lodge a petition at a place to be
specified by regulations made pursuant to this Act to prevent
the implementation of the law or regulations.

(2)   Where a petition has been lodged pursuant to subsection (1)

    (a)   the Secretary of State shall organise a referendum of
         all electors covered by the extent of the Act or
         Regulations on that petition; and

    (b)   if the referendum secures the support of a majority of
         those voting the Act or Regulations is repealed.

4)   Electors' right to initiate legislation

(1)   A Citizen's Bill is a Bill to which this section applies.

(2)   Parliamentary electors may by petition require the House
       of Commons to consider a 'Citizen's Bill' provided that no
       such requirement may be made more than once in any five-
       year period for the same Bill, or Bill with the same purpose.

(3)   In each session Parliament must make time for a Second
       Reading debate to be given to the six Citizen's Bills that
       secured the largest number of signatures on a petition in the
       previous session.

(4)   If any Citizen's Bill is given a Second Reading by the House
       of Commons it shall proceed as any other Bill and shall have
       equal priority to a government Bill to be considered by a
       Public Bill Committee and at any future stages in each
       House of Parliament, should the Bill proceed.

(5)   The organisers of any petition drawn up pursuant to
       subsection (1) may, with the agreement of the Member of
       Parliament concerned, nominate a Member of Parliament
       to promote their Bill and such Member shall be treated as
       the promoter of the Bill at Second Reading and any
       subsequent stages.

Appendix One
The Republican Contract with America

As Republican Members of the House of Representatives and as citizens seeking to join that body we propose not just to change its policies, but even more important, to restore the bonds of trust between the people and their elected representatives.

That is why, in this era of official evasion and posturing, we offer instead a detailed agenda for national renewal, a written commitment with no fine print.

This year's election offers the chance, after four decades of one-party control, to bring to the House a new majority that will transform the way Congress works. That historic change would be the end of government that is too big, too intrusive, and too easy with the public's money. It can be the beginning of a Congress that respects the values and shares the faith of the American family.

Like Lincoln, our first Republican president, we intend to act 'with firmness in the right, as God gives us to see the right.' To restore accountability to Congress. To end its cycle of scandal and disgrace. To make us all proud again of the way free people govern themselves.

On the first day of the 104th Congress, the new Republican majority will immediately pass the following major reforms, aimed at restoring the faith and trust of the American people in their government:

- FIRST, require all laws that apply to the rest of the country also apply equally to the Congress;
- SECOND, select a major, independent auditing firm to conduct a comprehensive audit of Congress for waste, fraud or abuse;
- THIRD, cut the number of House committees, and cut committee staff by one-third;
- FOURTH, limit the terms of all committee chairs;
- FIFTH, ban the casting of proxy votes in committee;
- SIXTH, require committee meetings to be open to the public;
- SEVENTH, require a three-fifths majority vote to pass a tax increase;

- EIGHTH, guarantee an honest accounting of our Federal Budget by implementing zero base-line budgeting.

Thereafter, within the first 100 days of the 104th Congress, we shall bring to the House Floor the following bills, each to be given full and open debate, each to be given a clear and fair vote and each to be immediately available this day for public inspection and scrutiny.

1. THE FISCAL RESPONSIBILITY ACT: A balanced budget/tax limitation amendment and a legislative line-item veto to restore fiscal responsibility to an out-of-control Congress, requiring them to live under the same budget constraints as families and businesses.
2. THE TAKING BACK OUR STREETS ACT: An anti-crime package including stronger truth-in-sentencing, 'good faith' exclusionary rule exemptions, effective death penalty provisions, and cuts in social spending from this summer's 'crime' bill to fund prison construction and additional law enforcement to keep people secure in their neighborhoods and kids safe in their schools.
3. THE PERSONAL RESPONSIBILITY ACT: Discourage illegitimacy and teen pregnancy by prohibiting welfare to minor mothers and denying increased AFDC for additional children while on welfare, cut spending for welfare programs, and enact a tough two-years-and-out provision with work requirements to promote individual responsibility.
4. THE FAMILY REINFORCEMENT ACT: Child support enforcement, tax incentives for adoption, strengthening rights of parents in their children's education, stronger child pornography laws, and an elderly dependent care tax credit to reinforce the central role of families in American society.
5. THE AMERICAN DREAM RESTORATION ACT: A $500 per child tax credit, begin repeal of the marriage tax penalty, and creation of American Dream Savings Accounts to provide middle class tax relief.
6. THE NATIONAL SECURITY RESTORATION ACT: No U.S. troops under U.N. command and restoration of the essential parts of

our national security funding to strengthen our national defense and maintain our credibility around the world.

7. THE SENIOR CITIZENS FAIRNESS ACT: Raise the Social Security earnings limit which currently forces seniors out of the work force, repeal the 1993 tax hikes on Social Security benefits and provide tax incentives for private long-term care insurance to let Older Americans keep more of what they have earned over the years.

8. THE JOB CREATION AND WAGE ENHANCEMENT ACT: Small business incentives, capital gains cut and indexation, neutral cost recovery, risk assessment/cost-benefit analysis, strengthening the Regulatory Flexibility Act and unfunded mandate reform to create jobs and raise worker wages.

9. THE COMMON SENSE LEGAL REFORM ACT: 'Loser pays' laws, reasonable limits on punitive damages and reform of product liability laws to stem the endless tide of litigation.

10. THE CITIZEN LEGISLATURE ACT: A first-ever vote on term limits to replace career politicians with citizen legislators.

Further, we will instruct the House Budget Committee to report to the floor and we will work to enact additional budget savings, beyond the budget cuts specifically included in the legislation described above, to ensure that the Federal budget deficit will be less than it would have been without the enactment of these bills.

Respecting the judgment of our fellow citizens as we seek their mandate for reform, we hereby pledge our names to this Contract with America.

Appendix Two:
Supporters of Direct Democracy

Adam Afriyie MP
Richard Benyon MP
Roger Bird
Fiona Bruce
Martin Callanan MEP
Douglas Carswell MP
Paul Carter
Greg Clark MP
Stephen Crabb MP
Iain Dale
Philip Dunne MP
Murdo Fraser MSP
David Gauke MP
Robert Goodwill MP
Michael Gove MP
Andrew Griffith
Robert Halfon
Stephen Hammond MP
Daniel Hannan MEP
Mark Harper MP
Chris Heaton-Harris MEP
Nick Herbert MP
Adam Holloway MP

Ed Howker
Jeremy Hunt MP
Stewart Jackson MP
Syed Kamall MEP
Scott Kelly
Danny Kruger
Kwasi Kwarteng
Julia Manning
Ali Miraj
Brian Monteith MSP
Brooks Newmark MP
Jesse Norman
Priti Patel
Mark Reckless
Ben Rogers
Laura Sandys
Janice Small
Henry Smith
James Sproule
Philippa Stroud
John Tate
Theresa Villiers MP

JS 113 .C37 2008
Carswell, Douglas.
The plan

Printed in the United States
218596BV00004B/9/P

9 780955 979903